The color book of
CROCKERY COOKING

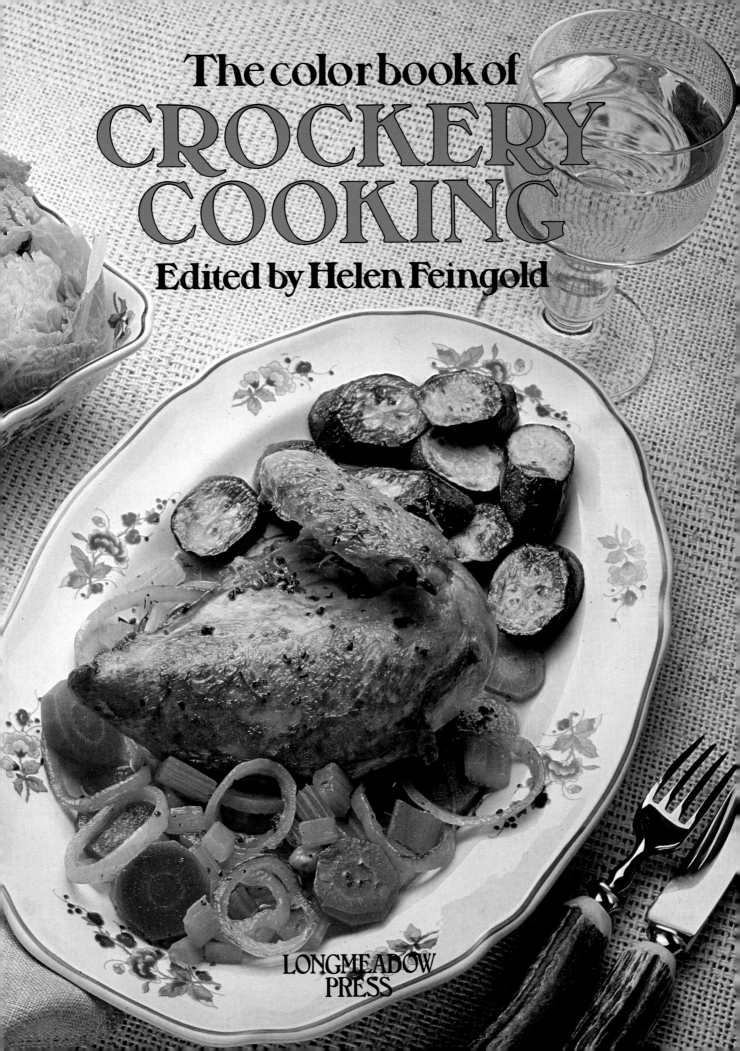

The color book of
CROCKERY COOKING

Edited by Helen Feingold

LONGMEADOW
PRESS

First published in the USA 1977 by
Longmeadow Press, PO Box 16
Rowayton Station, Norwalk, Connecticut 06853

© 1977 Octopus Books Limited

ISBN 0 7064 0687 7

Produced by Mandarin Publishers Limited
22a Westlands Road, Quarry Bay, Hong Kong

Printed in Hong Kong

Contents

Introduction 6
Broths, Soups and Sauces 10
Fish 18
Vegetables 30
Poultry and Game 40
Meat 52
Vegetarian 82
Desserts 90
Around the World 102
Entertaining 114
What Else? 120
Index 126

INTRODUCTION

Slow cooking is the modern approach to cooking foods by old-fashioned methods.

Over the centuries many different sources of heat have been used for cooking: a pit filled with hot bricks, an open fire or even a hay box. But always the accent has been on the slowness of cooking, to bring out the full flavor and complete tenderness in tough foods.

Slow cooking is easy and uncomplicated, especially suited to the busy lives most of us lead, where the time at home and that spent in the kitchen is at a premium. With the slow-cooking pot dishes can be prepared and left to cook unattended, all day or all night if you prefer. The slowness means that critical timing is not important, so if you are late home the food will not spoil.

The slow-cooking pot is economical too, only using as much fuel as an electric light bulb, and really tasty dishes can be prepared from the less expensive cuts of meat. Long slow cooking ensures tender, juicy meat and really delicious gravy. It also helps to retain more flavor, vitamins and minerals in the food.

The slow-cooking pot doesn't have to be confined to the kitchen. It makes an attractive party center piece with a hot punch, can be used in the dining room to serve the food straight from the pot, and is also ideal for buffet service on holidays.

Slow cooking means no turning, stirring, adjusting the heat or timing to the minute. It's versatile, too—steamed puddings, baked fish, soups and pâtés are just a few of the dishes you will discover as you read through this book. You are sure to find some new recipe ideas among the more familiar family favorites, all of which have been adapted to suit slow-cooking pots.

Before attempting any of the recipes in this book, read the information provided by the manufacturer of your slow-cooking pot. The recipes were designed for slow cookers having a removable stoneware pot, but can be adapted for use with other slow-cooking pots following the instructions on page 9 and the manufacturer's directions.

Using a slow cooking pot

The simplicity of the slow-cooking pot means that there is very little to learn about the appliance. However, there are a few points which ensure success every time.

Where you use the slow-cooking pot

An abnormally cold room or a direct draft will affect the cooking performance of the slow-cooking pot, particularly when using the low setting. If, however, these conditions are unavoidable it is better to use the high setting. Place pot on a level surface in a spot where it cannot be tipped or knocked off the counter. Place cord out of the way.

The two heat settings

Most recipes give the cooking times on either low (200°F.) or high (300°F.) so that you can select which is the more convenient. As slowness is the secret of the slow-cooking pot, low is given first as this allows for the longer cooking time.

However, some recipes achieve better results if cooked *only* on the high setting or conversely *only* on the low setting. These are clearly marked, as only one setting appears in the recipe.

As long as the overall recommended cooking time is allowed, the actual method of using the low and high settings can be adjusted as necessary: 1 hour on high is approximately equal to $2-2\frac{1}{2}$ hours on low. Every slow-cooking pot has different switches. Consult your use and care booklet. Make sure the pot is properly plugged in both at outlet and at pot.

Timing

As the slow-cooking pot cooks so very slowly, critical timing is not important. Foods left cooking longer than the recommended time will not spoil, burn or boil over. Most recipes indicate a cooking time showing two figures, e.g., low 8–10 hours. This means that after 8 hours the food will be cooked, but if you are not home, or are not ready for the meal, the slow-cooking pot will ensure that after 10 hours it will still be just as delicious to eat. At high altitudes it will be necessary to lengthen cooking times. Add 1–2 hours to cooking times.

Many timers are on the market that can be used to turn off the pot if you are delayed.

Removal of the lid during cooking

All recipes in this book, except YOGURT, must be cooked with the lid on.

The slowness of cooking means that stirring is hardly ever necessary and there is no need to keep looking at the food while it cooks. Once you have mixed the ingredients and started cooking, there is no need to remove the lid until you are ready to add ingredients toward the end of the cooking time, or serve the dish. Even occasional removal of the lid leads to considerable loss of heat and consequently cooking times have to be lengthened. The following are the only exceptions to this rule.
(a) Rice dishes cooked on high, where an occasional stir helps the even absorption of the liquid.
(b) When cooking on high for short periods, an occasional stir helps the distribution of flavors and keeps a sauce smooth, particularly if the 'liquid' is a can of soup.

Caring for your slow-cooking pot

Read the use and care booklet that comes with each slow-cooking pot to find out how to care for your pot whether it is made of crockery, stainless steel, glass, aluminum, baked enamel or is lined with teflon.

Choosing and preparing foods

The special characteristics of slow-cooking mean that some foods require slightly different preparation from usual.

Vegetables

Use less of the stronger flavored vegetables.

Vegetables must be sliced or diced and generally placed *under* meats.

See vegetable section (page 30).

Meat

It is best if meat is pre-browned; this *must* be done in a separate pan unless you have a slow-cooking pot with a variable heat control, then the browning can be done in the pot at 400°F. The temperature is then lowered for slow cooking to 200°F. or 300°F.

See poultry and meat sections (pages 40 and 52) for more detailed information.

Liquid

Generally $1\frac{1}{4}$ cups liquid is enough for cooking, unless otherwise stated. Cooking liquid can be water, broth, wine or soup, but not milk or cream as both of these break down during long cooking. Milk should be added toward the end of the cooking and cream at the completion of cooking.

Herbs and spices

As maximum flavors are retained during cooking, less herbs, spices and flavorings are required. If using one of your own recipes, reduce the amount you normally use by half.

Cheese

Generally, processed cheeses are more satisfactory for long cooking. Hard cheeses are better grated than sliced.

Pasta

Pasta should be cooked to 'al dente' (just soft), and rinsed in hot water before being added to the slow-cooking pot.

Rice

For savory dishes the pre-cooked variety is recommended.

Soup

Canned or dehydrated soups are extremely useful to use as the cooking liquid. Condensed soups are very satisfactory and can be used undiluted. Dehydrated soups should be cooked with only half the recommended quantity of water. Both require a thorough stir at the completion of cooking.

See soup section (page 10).

Thickening sauce and gravy

Always do this at the completion of cooking. All-purpose flour or cornstarch are suggested in the recipes. These should be dissolved in a little of the cooking liquid and stirred in about half-an-hour before you wish to serve the dish.

The recipes

Most of the recipes in this book are intended to serve 4–6 people and were tested in a slow-cooking pot with a capacity of 8 cups (2 quarts). If your pot is bigger, recipes may be doubled or otherwise increased for the capacity of your pot.

Cooking times may be slightly shorter when smaller quantities are used. The times shown are only applicable when the pot is at least half-filled.

If the recipe is reduced by half it is better to keep the amount of liquid used at $\frac{2}{3}$ cup.

The slow-cooking pot or stoneware pot should not be filled above the rim and the lid must sit easily in place.

Varieties of slow-cooking pots

Manufacturer	Temperature control	Usable capacity	How to change recipes
Corning Electromatic Table Range	200°F.–500°F.	2½ quart casserole/lid	Use same recipe and cooking time.
	240°F.–Low 350°F.–High	4½ quart dutch oven/lid	Double recipe and same cooking time.
Dominion	Low–High Cooks cooler Glass liner	3 quarts	Same recipe but lengthen cooking time 10%.
Farberware	Low–High Removable stoneware pot	3 quarts	Same recipe or 1½ times recipe. Same cooking time.
Grandinetti	Low–High Removable stoneware pot	3 quarts	*Same recipe or increase to 1½ times recipe.
		3½ quarts	*Same recipe or increase to 1½ times recipe.
		4 quarts	*Double recipe. *Same cooking time for all.
Hamilton Beach	Low–High Removable crockery pot	3 quarts	Same recipe or 1½ times recipe. Same cooking time.
Oster Cooker/fryer	200°F.–500°F. Cooks hotter Metal pot 200°F.–Low 300°F.–High	7 quarts	Triple recipe. Reduce cooking time by 10%.
Penny's Cooker/fryer	200°–500°F. 200°F.–Low 325°F.–High Cooks hotter	4 quarts	Double recipe. Same cooking time.
Slow-cooker	Low–High Metal pot	3 quarts	Same recipe or 1½ times recipe. Reduce cooking time by 10%.
Regal Poly Pot	Low–High Teflon metal	5 quarts	Double recipe. Same cooking time.
Reliable	Low–High Cooks hotter	5 quarts	Double recipe. Reduce cooking time by 10%.
Rival	Low–High Removable stoneware pot	2½ quarts 3 quarts 4 quarts	*Same recipe. *1½ times recipe. *Double recipe. *Same cooking time for all.
Sears	Med.–(Low) High Removable crockery pot	3½ quarts	Same recipe or increase to 1½ times recipe. Same cooking time.
Sunbeam Slow-cooker	Red light–200 watts Amber light–100 watts Removable crockery pot	3 quarts	1½ times recipe. Same cooking time.
Cooker/fryer	280°F.–420°F. 280°F.–Low 325°F.–High Cooks hotter Removable crockery pot	4 quarts 4 quarts	Double recipe. Same cooking time. Double recipe. Reduce cooking time 10%.
Sunbeam Slow-cooker Frypan	280°F.–420°F. 280°F.–Low 325°F.–High Cooks hotter Removable crockery pot	3 quarts	1½ times recipe. Reduce cooking time 10%.
Wearever	Low–High Removable crockery pot	3 quarts 5 quarts	Same recipe or 1½ times recipe. Same cooking time. Double recipe. Same cooking time.
West Bend	Low–High Use only High setting Removable stoneware pot	2 quarts	Same recipe but lengthen cooking time 10%.
	5 heat setting 2–Low 5–High Metal pot	3½ quarts 5 quarts	*1½ times recipe. *Double recipe. *Same cooking time.

BROTHS, SOUPS AND SAUCES

There is nothing quite so satisfying as a bowl of hot soup on a cold day and it is doubly satisfying if it is home-made. Soups are ideally suited to cook during the night, leaving the slow-cooking pot free during the daytime to cook for the evening meal. A chicken or turkey carcass need never be wasted—cooked with a few vegetables it makes a delicious soup. Noodles or small dumplings can also be added to make a soup into a meal.

Soup recipes often require 5—7½ cups water. In the slow-cooking pot this amount is not generally necessary: put all the ingredients into the pot and add enough water just to cover them. The consistency of the soup can be adjusted at the completion of cooking, particularly for a soup that is to be puréed or put through a blender before it is served. Milk or cream must always be added at the end of the cooking time as both separate and break down during the long, slow cooking.

If you have meat or poultry bones it is worthwhile making them into basic broths. Once cooked, cool quickly, refrigerate, remove hardened fat, chill or freeze until needed. Fish broth is best used within 24 hours. Broths, like soups, are ideally suited to cook overnight. When preparing the ingredients, use less of the strong-flavored vegetables such as onions, celery or turnips than usual, as the long, slow cooking draws out all their flavors. Add just enough liquid to cover or, for a more concentrated broth, use less liquid and seal between the pot and its lid with foil.

All broths can be cooked on low for 12—16 hours or high for 6 hours.

The sauces in this section show how the slow-cooking pot can help in preparing the most important ingredient of some recipes, so that when the time comes to prepare a dish it is only a matter of minutes instead of hours. If you own a freezer, larger quantities may be prepared at one time then divided into suitable family servings and frozen.

Opposite: Italian vegetable soup (page 14)

Meat broth (brown)

2–3lbs. raw or cooked bones (lamb, beef, pork, etc.)
I medium-sized onion, sliced
½ small yellow turnip, sliced
2 carrots, sliced
I rib celery, chopped
I teaspoon salt
small bouquet garni (parsley, thyme, bay leaf,
    tarragon)
water to cover

For a really brown stock, brown the bones and the
onion in 2 tablespoons hot fat in a frying pan before
transferring to the slow-cooking pot. Add remaining
ingredients. Cover and cook on low or high. Strain.

Low   8–10 hours
High 4–5 hours

Chicken broth (white)

Use same amount of chicken carcass, skin and giblets
    instead of meat bones.

Prepare as for Meat broth (brown).

Fish broth

2–3lbs. fish trimmings (bones, head, tail, skin)
small bouquet garni (bay leaf, parsley, dill)
4 white peppercorns
a pinch of salt
I small onion, sliced
piece of lemon rind
water to cover

Fish broth is best used within 24 hours. Time same as
for Meat broth (brown).

Leek and potato soup

2 leeks, white part only, sliced
Ilb. potatoes, sliced
2 tablespoons margarine
salt and pepper
2 cups chicken broth or water
2 egg yolks mixed with 3 tablespoons milk or cream
finely chopped green from leeks, to garnish

Pack the slow-cooking pot with the vegetables,
margarine, salt and pepper and broth. Cover and cook
on low or high. Half-an-hour before serving, mash the

vegetables into the liquid, stir in the egg yolks and
milk or cream with additional liquid to thin the soup
if required. Continue cooking on low until slightly
thickened. Just before serving sprinkle with finely
chopped leeks.

Low   8–10 hours
High 4–5 hours

Split pea and ham soup

4 slices bacon, chopped
ham bone, washed
I leek, sliced
I rib celery, chopped
½ cup split peas (pre-soak 4–5 hours before use)
bay leaf
pinch of nutmeg
salt and pepper
2½ cups water

Fry the bacon gently in a separate pan until
half-cooked. Add with remaining ingredients to the
slow-cooking pot. Cover and cook on low. To serve,
lift out the ham bone and bay leaf, mash the
vegetables into the liquid and add more water, if
necessary. Season again with salt and pepper.

Low   overnight (minimum 10–12 hours)

Country vegetable soup

2 medium-sized potatoes, peeled
2 carrots, scraped
2 ribs celery
I small parsnip, peeled
I small white turnip, peeled
I small onion, peeled
salt and pepper
2½ cups chicken broth or water
3 tablespoons peas

Cut all the vegetables (except the peas) into small
cubes. Put into the slow-cooking pot, season with
salt and pepper and add the liquid. Cover and cook
on low or high. Half-an-hour before serving, stir in
the peas. (If fresh peas are used, these may be added
at the beginning with all the other ingredients.)
Add more water, if necessary. Season again.

Low   10–12 hours, or overnight
High 5–6 hours

Cream of tomato soup

1½lbs. tomatoes
2 tablespoons butter
1 small onion, chopped
2 carrots, thinly sliced
2 ribs celery, chopped
2 slices bacon, chopped
bouquet garni (basil, thyme, parsley)
2½ cups chicken broth or water
1 teaspoon sugar
salt and pepper
milk
3 tablespoons light cream

Skin the tomatoes by placing them in boiling water for 1 minute. Core and cut them into quarters. Melt the butter in a separate pan and lightly sauté the onion, carrot, celery and bacon. Transfer to the slow-cooking pot with the tomatoes, bouquet garni, broth, sugar and salt and pepper. Cover and cook on low or high. When cooked, press the soup through a strainer back into the rinsed slow-cooking pot. Add milk until the right consistency. Add the cream just before serving.

Low   8–10 hours
High 4–5 hours

French onion soup

1lb. onions, sliced
¼ cup butter
3 tablespoons oil
1 teaspoon salt
1 teaspoon sugar
¼ cup all-purpose flour
2½ cups beef broth
salt and pepper
French bread
grated cheese

In a separate pan, fry the onions in the butter and oil. After 2-3 minutes, add the salt and sugar and continue cooking until the onions are light golden brown. Transfer to the slow-cooking pot. Stir the flour into the juices in the pan, remove from heat and pour in the broth, stirring continuously. Pour over the onions and season with salt and pepper. Cover and cook on low or high. Just before serving, add thick rounds of toasted French bread topped with grated cheese, melted under the broiler.

Low   6–8 hours
High 3–4 hours

Minestrone

3 slices bacon, chopped
I small onion, sliced
I small leek, trimmed and chopped
2 tablespoons butter or margarine
I clove garlic, crushed
few sprigs parsley
½ small green cabbage, cored and shredded
I medium-sized potato, peeled and diced
I cup I-inch pieces green beans
2 ribs celery, diced
2 small carrots, thinly sliced
¼ cup pre-cooked long grain rice
salt and pepper
3 cups chicken broth or water

Brown the bacon, onion and leek in the butter in a skillet. Drain excess fat. Add with all the other ingredients to the slow-cooking pot. Stir well. Cover and cook on low.

Low   10–12 hours or overnight

Seafood chowder

1½lbs. fresh or frozen fillets of cod or haddock
4 slices bacon, chopped
I onion, sliced
2 medium-sized potatoes, peeled and diced
salt and pepper
1¼ cups fish broth
⅔ cup milk
½ cup cooked, shelled and deveined shrimp

Cut the trimmed fish into I-inch pieces (if frozen allow to thaw). In a separate pan, fry the bacon until crisp, add the onion and sauté until transparent. Place the vegetables and the bacon in the slow-cooking pot, add the fish, salt and pepper and broth. Cover and cook on low or high. Half-an-hour before serving, stir in the milk and shrimp. Serve with crisp French bread.

Low   6–8 hours
High   3–4 hours

Italian vegetable soup

½lb. beef shank or stew meat
3 cups water
I onion, chopped
I teaspoon salt
I teaspoon powdered thyme
2 tablespoons chopped parsley
¼ teaspoon pepper
I can (8oz.) tomatoes, cut up
I rib celery, diced
I carrot, diced
I leek, sliced
I can (8oz.) pinto beans, drained
I cup chopped green cabbage
½ cup small macaroni, uncooked
I slice bacon, chopped
¼ cup grated Parmesan cheese

In slow-cooking pot combine beef with water, onion salt, thyme, parsley, pepper and tomatoes. Cover and cook on low. Remove beef bones; cut up meat and return to pot. Turn control to high. Add celery, carrots, leek, beans, cabbage, macaroni and bacon. Cover and cook on high until vegetables are tender. Sprinkle with cheese.

Low   7–9 hours
High   30–45 minutes

Iced cucumber soup

2 cucumbers
I small onion, finely chopped
3¾ cups chicken broth
sprig of mint
I teaspoon arrowroot
⅔ cup light cream or half-and-half
salt and pepper
a little green food coloring
sprig of mint to garnish

Peel and chop the cucumbers, reserving a little for garnish. Place the cucumber, onion, broth and mint in slow-cooking pot. Cover and cook on low or high. When cooked, press soup through a strainer or whirl in a blender and return it to the rinsed pot. Turn to high. Mix the arrowroot with the cream, stir thoroughly into soup and heat until thickened. Add a little green food coloring. Cool soup, then chill before serving. Garnish with additional diced cucumber and a sprig of mint.

Low 4–6 hours
High 2–3 hours

Cream of celery soup

2 tablespoons butter or margarine
I bunch celery, finely chopped (reserve a few of the best leaves for garnish)
I small onion, finely chopped
2½ cups chicken broth or water
salt and pepper
3 tablespoons light cream

Heat the butter or margarine in a separate pan. Sauté celery and onion in this for a few minutes. Drain and transfer to the slow-cooking pot with the broth and salt and pepper. Cover and cook on low or high. When cooked, press the ingredients through a strainer or whirl in blender. Return the soup to the pot and add more broth if necessary. Check seasoning. Just before serving, stir in the cream and garnish with finely chopped celery leaves.

Low 7–9 hours
High 3½–4½ hours

Scotch broth

Ilb. lamb neck or shoulder
3¾ cups water
2 onions, finely chopped
I cup finely chopped carrots
I cup finely chopped turnips
2 leeks, thinly sliced
¼ cup fine barley
salt and pepper
chopped parsley to garnish

Place the meat in a saucepan with the water, bring to a boil and skim. Place the vegetables and barley in the slow-cooking pot. Season with salt and pepper. Place the meat on top and add the hot cooking liquid. Cover and cook on low or high. Lift out the lamb, remove from bone and cut into small pieces. Return meat to the slow-cooking pot, adjust seasoning and

Below: Scotch broth

add more liquid if required. Serve sprinkled with chopped parsley.

Low 9–11 hours } plus ½ hour on high if more
High 4½–5½ hours } liquid added

Mulligatawny

I cooking apple, peeled, cored and sliced
I onion, sliced
2 carrots, sliced
¼ cup butter
3 tablespoons curry powder
¼ cup all-purpose flour
5 cups chicken broth
2 chicken quarters, about 1½lbs.
few drops lemon juice

Sauté the apple, onion and carrot in butter in a separate pan. Add the curry powder. Stir in the flour and broth and bring to a boil. Pour into slow-cooking pot. Add the chicken, cover and cook on low or high. Remove the chicken and press the soup through a strainer or whirl in a blender. Slice the chicken meat and add to the soup with the lemon juice. Reheat.

Low 8–10 hours
High 4–5 hours

Borscht

1lb. cooked beets, diced
1 onion, finely diced
2 carrots, finely sliced
1 large potato, finely diced
2 parsnips, finely diced
2 ribs celery, finely sliced
3¾ cups beef or chicken broth
bay leaf
1 tablespoon tomato paste
salt and pepper
⅔ cup sour cream
1 tablespoon chopped parsley to garnish

Place the vegetables in the slow-cooking pot with the broth, bay leaf, tomato paste and salt and pepper. Cover and cook on low or high. Purée the soup in a blender or press through a strainer. Add more broth or water until the correct consistency. Just before serving, stir in the sour cream and sprinkle with chopped parsley.
    Makes approximately 5 pints.

Low   10–12 hours
High   5–6 hours

Cock-a-leekie

4 leeks, split and sliced
6 prunes, pitted
2 chicken quarters (about 1½lbs.)
salt and pepper
3¾ cups hot chicken broth
1 tablespoon pre-cooked rice

Place all the ingredients except the rice in the slow-cooking pot. Cover and cook on low. Add the rice, stir well and continue cooking for a further hour. During this time, remove the chicken from the soup, remove skin and bones, chop meat and return it to the soup. Season to taste with salt and pepper.

Low   8–10 hours

Lentil soup

¾ cup lentils
1 clove garlic, crushed
1 large onion, sliced
1 carrot, diced
2 ribs celery, sliced
2 tomatoes, chopped
½lb. bacon, diced
¼ teaspoon dried marjoram

salt and pepper
3¾ cups beef broth

Wash the lentils, place in the slow-cooking pot, just cover with cold salted water, cover and cook on low overnight. Drain off any surplus liquid. Add the garlic, onion, carrot, celery, tomatoes, bacon, marjoram, salt, pepper and broth, cover and cook on low. Skim excess fat. Add more broth, if necessary.

Low   8–10 hours

Chicken noodle soup

1 chicken carcass, broken into several pieces
1 onion, finely chopped
2 ribs celery, finely chopped
bay leaf
few sprigs parsley
pinch of thyme
3¾ cups water or chicken broth
1 cup fine noodles
2 teaspoons chopped parsley

Put all the ingredients, except the noodles and parsley, in the slow-cooking pot. Cover and cook on low. Remove the carcass and cut off any meat. Return to pot with noodles and parsley, cover and cook on low. Remove bay leaf before serving.
    (A turkey carcass may be used instead.)

Low   8–10 hours (or overnight),
        plus 1 hour (for noodles)

Curry sauce

¼ cup lard or drippings
2 medium-sized onions, chopped
3 tablespoons curry powder (to taste)
3 tablespoons all-purpose flour
2½ cups beef broth
3 tablespoons tomato paste
3 tablespoons chutney
4 teaspoons lemon juice
½ cup yellow raisins
salt

Melt the fat in a separate pan and sauté onion. Add the curry powder and flour and cook for 2–3 minutes. Remove from heat, gradually stir in the broth and remaining ingredients. Transfer to the slow-cooking pot, cover and cook on low. Any cooked meats or fish may be added to this sauce during the last half-hour of cooking, which should then be completed on high. The long, slow cooking of this sauce enables the curry spices to combine thoroughly.

Low   4–6 hours

Tomato sauce

1½ lbs. tomatoes
2 tablespoons butter
1 small onion, chopped
2 carrots, thinly sliced
2 ribs celery, chopped
2 slices bacon, chopped
bay leaf
a few peppercorns
a few parsley stalks
2½ cups chicken broth or water
salt and pepper
3 tablespoons all-purpose flour mixed with
    ¼ cup water

Skin the tomatoes by placing them in boiling water
for 1 minute. Core and cut into quarters. Melt the
butter in a separate pan and lightly sauté the onion,
carrot, celery and bacon. Transfer to the slow-cooking
pot with the tomatoes, bay leaf, peppercorns, parsley
stalks, broth and salt and pepper. Cover and cook on
low or high. When cooked, press the sauce through a
strainer back into the rinsed slow-cooking pot. Stir in
the flour mixture and cook for a further 30 minutes.

Low   8–10 hours, plus
High   4–5 hours, plus

Bolognese sauce

1 lb. ground chuck
1 medium-sized onion, chopped
2 tablespoons lard
½ cup chopped mushrooms
1 can (16oz.) tomatoes
bay leaf
salt and pepper
pinch of fines herbes
2 tablespoons red wine

Quickly fry the chuck and onion in the lard in a
separate pan. Transfer to the slow-cooking pot with
remaining ingredients and stir well. Cover and cook
on low or high. Serve with spaghetti which should be
cooked in briskly boiling water for 10–12 minutes.
Drain well, place on a heated serving dish and pour
the Bolognese sauce over spaghetti. Remove bay leaf
before serving.

Low   6–8 hours
High   3–4 hours

Below: Bolognese sauce

Espagnole sauce

¼ cup butter
6 slices bacon, chopped
2 small onions, chopped
2 carrots, sliced
1 cup chopped mushrooms
½ cup all-purpose flour
⅓ cup tomato paste
5 cups beef broth
salt and pepper
⅓ cup sherry

Melt the butter in a separate pan and fry the bacon,
onion, carrots and mushrooms until golden. Drain
well and transfer to the slow-cooking pot. Stir the
flour into fat and juices in the pan. Fry until lightly
browned, remove from heat, stir in the tomato paste
and broth, then season with salt and pepper. Pour
over the vegetables. Cover and cook on low. When
cooked, press through a strainer and stir in the sherry.
Use as required.

Low   6–8 hours

FISH

Like the less expensive meats, the less expensive fish can also be put to good use in the slow-cooking pot.

Mackerel, turbot and whiting make interesting, appetizing meals full of protein and flavor. Cooked slowly, the flesh stays firm while the bones just lift out.

A fish casserole, using a can of condensed soup as the sauce, makes a quickly prepared dish, see Mock-lobster casserole (page 24). This is an ideal way of dressing up plain fish into something special. And with the slow cooking pot, the aroma will be held in until you lift the lid to serve the meal.

Fish has softer flesh than meat, and this is reflected in the shorter cooking times recommended.

All frozen fish MUST be thoroughly thawed before cooking commences and fresh fish should be cooked on the day or day after purchase.

Opposite: Baked avocado with crab (page 23)

Continental fish casserole

1½lbs. cod or haddock fillets
1 small onion, chopped
½lb. zucchini, thinly sliced
salt and pepper
bay leaf
bouquet garni (dill, thyme, bay leaf)
1 can (16oz.) tomatoes

Wash and dry the fish, divide into four portions. Place the onion and zucchini in the slow-cooking pot, put the fish on top and add salt and pepper and herbs. Add the tomatoes roughly chopped. Cover and cook on low or high. Remove bay leaf before serving.

Low   6–8 hours
High   3–4 hours

Soused herrings

6 fresh herrings, cleaned and boned
salt and pepper
1 small onion, thinly sliced
few peppercorns
few sprigs parsley
2 bay leaves
⅔ cup malt vinegar
⅔ cup water

Remove the head, tail and fins from the herrings. Season with salt and pepper and roll up from head end. Pack into the slow-cooking pot with remaining ingredients. Cover and cook on low or high. Remove bay leaves before serving.

Low   6–8 hours
High   3–4 hours

Rice stuffed cod

1½lbs. cod fillet
¼ cup cooked long grain rice
2 ribs celery, finely chopped
2 navel oranges
salt and pepper
bay leaf
⅔ cup fish broth or water

Cut fillet into 2 equal pieces. Mix together the rice, celery, juice and pulp from one of the oranges and salt and pepper. Spoon filling on 1 piece of cod and top with second piece. Secure with string tied at intervals.

Place in the slow-cooking pot with the bay leaf and liquid. Remove the rind from the second orange, cut into slices and arrange along top of fish. Cover and cook on low or high. Remove string before serving.

Low   6–8 hours
High   3–4 hours

Curried shrimp

Curry Sauce as given on page 16
1lb. shelled and deveined shrimp

Prepare and cook the curry sauce as given on page 16 adding the shrimp during the last half hour of cooking. Serve on a bed of cooked long grain rice with lemon wedges.

Butter baked whiting

4 whiting
1 cup herb stuffing mix mixed with ¼ cup water
2 tablespoons butter
1 tablespoon Worcestershire sauce
4 sprigs parsley

Have the fish cleaned, removing head and tail. Dry on absorbent paper towels. Fill the cavity of the fish with the stuffing. Sew or skewer opening. Use a little of the butter to grease the slow-cooking pot. Add the fish, laying them head to tail, pour a few drops of Worcestershire sauce over each fish and cover with the remaining butter cut into small pieces. Lay the parsley sprigs on top. Cover and cook on low or high.

Low   4–6 hours
High   2–3 hours

Tuna and corn savory

1 can (7oz.) tuna fish
1 can (12oz.) kernel corn
little butter for greasing
1 cup (4oz.) grated cheese
1 tablespoon chopped parsley
salt and pepper
2 eggs
⅔ cup milk

Drain the tuna fish and corn. Transfer to the lightly greased slow-cooking pot and mix with three-quarters of the cheese, the parsley and salt and pepper. Beat the eggs in a measuring cup and add enough milk to make I cup. Pour evenly over the other ingredients. Cover and cook on low or high. Sprinkle with the remaining cheese. Serve as a supper dish with sliced tomato and green salad.

Low   4–6 hours
High   2–3 hours

Flounder parcels

4 flounder fillets
2 tablespoons butter
½ cup chopped mushrooms
½ cup chopped shrimp
salt and pepper
6 tablespoons fish broth or water
bay leaf
few sprigs of parsley

Sauce
milk
I tablespoon butter
I tablespoon all-purpose flour

Wash flounder and pat dry. Grease the slow-cooking pot with butter and place two of the fillets side-by-side in pot. Dot with butter, add to each one a mixture of the mushrooms and shrimp and season with salt and pepper. Place the remaining two fillets on top. Pour the liquid around them, adding the bay leaf and parsley. Cover and cook on low. When cooked, strain the liquid into a measuring cup and add enough milk to make I cup. Melt the butter in a saucepan and stir in the flour. Cook for I minute. Remove from the heat and gradually stir in the liquid. Return to heat, bring to a boil and adjust seasoning with salt and pepper. Pour over flounder parcels.

Low 4–6 hours

Lemon mackerel

4 mackerel
I cup fine soft breadcrumbs
grated rind of I lemon
I teaspoon chopped parsley
½ teaspoon fines herbes
3 tablespoons milk
2 tablespoons butter
salt and pepper
juice of I lemon

Have fish cleaned, removing head and tail. Dry on absorbent paper towels. Mix the breadcrumbs, lemon

rind, herbs and milk. With the mixture, stuff the cavity of the fish and secure the opening with toothpicks. Grease the slow-cooking pot with the butter and put in the fish, laying them head to tail. Season with salt and pepper and pour over the lemon juice. Cover and cook on low or high.

Serve with lemon wedges and whole wheat bread and butter.

Low   4–6 hours
High   2–3 hours

Red snapper with orange

4 small red snapper fillets
butter
2 navel oranges
½ teaspoon dill
salt and pepper
I teaspoon cornstarch

Rinse the fillets and dry thoroughly. Place in the greased slow-cooking pot. Add the juice and grated rind of I orange, dill and salt and pepper. Slice the other orange thinly and place over fish, slightly overlapping. Cover and cook on low or high. Drain pan juices into a saucepan and thicken with cornstarch. Serve sauce over fish.

Low   3–5 hours
High   1½–2½ hours

21

Deviled herrings

4–6 fresh herrings
salt and pepper
3 tablespoons all-purpose flour
3 tablespoons dry mustard
⅔ cup boiling water

Have herring cleaned and scaled and remove head,
fins and tail. Wash. Lay the fish, head to tail, in the
slow-cooking pot, season with salt and pepper. Mix
together the flour and mustard and stir in a little
cold water to form a smooth paste. Gradually add the
boiling water, stirring continuously. Pour over the
herrings. Cook on low or high. Remove fish. Stir
sauce well and pour over herring.

Low   4–6 hours
High   2–3 hours

Tuna loaf

1 can (7oz.) tuna
2 cups soft white breadcrumbs
large pinch of nutmeg
salt and pepper
⅔ cup milk
1 egg, beaten

4 tomatoes, sliced
1 cup (4oz.) grated Cheddar cheese

Mix the flaked fish, breadcrumbs, nutmeg, salt,
pepper, milk and egg. Place a layer of tomatoes in the
bottom of a lightly greased 1-lb loaf pan, followed by a
layer of the cheese and a layer of the fish mixture.
Repeat the layers once more. Cover with greased
aluminum foil and place in the slow-cooking pot with
1 cup water around it. Cover and cook on low or
high. Serve hot or cold with green salad.

Low   4–6 hours
High   2–3 hours

Mackerel loaf

4 small mackerel, skinned and filleted
2 teaspoons lemon juice
1 teaspoon fines herbes
large pinch nutmeg
1 cup cooked long grain rice
3 hard-cooked eggs, chopped
½ cup sliced mushrooms
1 egg, beaten
salt and pepper

Marinate the mackerel fillets in a mixture of lemon
juice, herbs and nutmeg for 1 hour. Chop two of the

fillets and mix with the rice, eggs and mushrooms. Add the beaten egg, salt and pepper. Place half of this mixture in a greased I quart casserole. Arrange the fish fillets on top and cover with the remaining mixture. Cover with greased aluminum foil. Stand the container in the slow-cooking pot with I cup water around it. Cover and cook on low or high. If serving cold, leave to cool in the casserole. Loosen edges and turn out.

Low   4–6 hours
High   2–3 hours

Flounder bonne femme

4 flounder fillets
$\frac{3}{4}$ cup sliced button mushrooms
$\frac{2}{3}$ cup white wine
$1\frac{1}{4}$ cups milk
2 tablespoons butter
$\frac{1}{4}$ cup all-purpose flour
salt and pepper

Wash and dry the fillets. Place half of the mushrooms on one-half of each fillet, then fold the fillet in half. Place in the slow-cooking pot with the wine and cook on low. Cook the remaining mushrooms in $\frac{1}{4}$ cup of the milk, reserving the rest of the milk for the sauce. When the flounder is cooked, strain the cooking liquid, reserving $\frac{1}{2}$ cup. Melt the butter in a saucepan, stir in the flour and cook for I minute. Remove from heat and gradually stir in the reserved liquids and mushrooms. Return to the heat, bring to a boil and add salt and pepper to taste. Pour over the flounder.

Low   2–3 hours

Baked avocado with crab

3 tomatoes
$\frac{2}{3}$ cup white sauce
3 tablespoons tomato paste
pinch of nutmeg
I cup crab meat
2 ripe avocados
salt and pepper
lemon juice
$\frac{1}{3}$ cup water

Skin the tomatoes by placing in boiling water for I minute, cut into quarters. Remove the seeds and

slice. Add to the white sauce with the tomato paste, nutmeg and flaked crab meat and stir to mix. Cut the avocados in half lengthwise and remove the seeds. Sprinkle with salt, pepper, and lemon juice to prevent discoloring. Pile the crab mixture into the avocado halves and arrange in slow-cooking pot. Pour water around them. Cover and cook on low.

Low   2–3 hours

Fish pie

$1\frac{1}{2}$lbs. cod or haddock fillets
I small onion, chopped
$\frac{1}{4}$lb. button mushrooms
salt and pepper
2 sprigs parsley
bay leaf
$\frac{2}{3}$ cup chicken broth or water
2 tablespoons margarine or butter
$\frac{1}{4}$ cup all-purpose flour
$1\frac{1}{4}$ cups milk
2 eggs, hard-cooked and quartered
2lbs. potatoes, cooked and mashed
I teaspoon chopped parsley

Cut the fish into I-inch cubes and place in the slow-cooking pot with the onion, mushrooms, salt and pepper and herbs. Add the broth, cover and cook on low or high. Strain the liquid, reserving $\frac{1}{2}$ cup for the sauce. Melt the fat in a saucepan, stir in the flour and cook gently for I minute. Remove from heat and gradually stir in liquid and milk. Return to heat and bring to a boil, stirring continuously. Season to taste

with salt and pepper. Pour fish into a 1-quart casserole. Gently stir the eggs into the fish and pour the sauce over. Mix the potato and parsley and either spread or pipe over the fish. Brown in a hot oven or under the broiler.

Low   4–6 hours
High   2–3 hours

NOTE: If you have a stoneware pot, leave fish and sauce in pot, cover with mashed potatoes. Remove stoneware pot from base and place in oven as above.

Mock-lobster casserole

1½lbs. cod fillets
1 small onion, finely chopped
¼lb. button mushrooms
1 tablespoon chopped parsley
salt and pepper
2 cans (10¾oz. each) condensed cream of shrimp soup

Cut the fish into large cubes. (If using frozen fish, thaw thoroughly.) Combine with the remaining ingredients in the slow-cooking pot and stir thoroughly. Cover and cook on low or high.

Low   5–6 hours
High   2½–3 hours

Mediterranean mullet

2 tablespoons butter or margarine
2 tomatoes
1 small green pepper, seeded and sliced
1 cup sliced mushrooms
salt and pepper
4 medium-sized red mullet or bluefish
⅓ cup red wine
few chopped chives

Use half the butter to grease the slow-cooking pot. Skin the tomatoes by placing them in boiling water for 1 minute, then slice. Mix the vegetables together and place in the pot with a little salt and pepper. Wash fish carefully, remove fins and trim tails. Place the fish on top of the vegetables, laying them head to tail. Pour over the wine and a little more salt and pepper. Dot with the remaining butter and sprinkle lightly with the chopped chives. Cover and cook on low or high.

Low   4–6 hours
High   2–3 hours

Baked trout with almonds

4 trout
salt and pepper
¼ cup butter
juice of 1 lemon
½ cup sliced almonds

Have trout cleaned and remove heads. Season inside and out with salt and pepper. Use a little of the butter to grease the slow-cooking pot, then add the fish, laying them head to tail. Sprinkle with the lemon juice and almonds, then cover with the butter cut into small pieces. Cover and cook on low or high.

Low   4–6 hours
High   2–3 hours

Tomato and mackerel bake

4 mackerel
salt and pepper
1 small onion, finely chopped
1 clove garlic, crushed
6 firm tomatoes, skinned and sliced
2 tablespoons butter
1 teaspoon chopped parsley

Have the fish cleaned and remove heads and tails. Season inside and out with salt and pepper. Put a layer of onion, garlic and tomatoes over the bottom of the greased slow-cooking pot. Add the fish, laying them head to tail. Dot with butter and sprinkle with parsley. Cover and cook on low or high.

Low   4–6 hours
High   2–3 hours

Cheesy fish bake

2 tablespoons butter or margarine
1½lbs. cod or haddock fillets
1 small onion, finely chopped
1 cup (4oz.) grated cheese
salt and pepper
⅔ cup hard cider
2 cups soft white breadcrumbs

Grease the slow-cooking pot well with butter. Cut the fish into cubes and dry well. Put the fish, onion

and half the cheese into the pot, season with salt and pepper and mix thoroughly. Add the cider. Cover and cook on low or high. Pour into a heatproof serving platter. Sprinkle with remaining cheese and crumbs. Place under broiler until top is browned.

Low   6–8 hours
High   3–4 hours

NOTE: If you have a stoneware pot, leave fish in pot and sprinkle with cheese and crumbs. Broil as above after removing from base.

Kedgeree

½ lb. raw smoked haddock
2 hard-cooked eggs, chopped
I cup pre-cooked long grain rice
I tablespoon chopped parsley
2 cups cold chicken broth or water
salt and pepper to taste

Chop the fish into small pieces. Mix together all the ingredients in the slow-cooking pot. Cover and cook on low or high.

Low   6–8 hours
High   3–4 hours

Tuna pilaf

I small green pepper, seeded and chopped
2 ribs celery, finely chopped
I package (10oz.) frozen kernel corn, thawed
I cup pre-cooked long grain rice
I tablespoon chopped parsley
salt and pepper
I can (7oz.) tuna fish
2 cups cold chicken broth or water
lemon wedges to garnish

Mix the pepper, celery, corn, rice, parsley and salt and pepper in the slow-cooking pot. Drain the tuna and flake. Stir into the other ingredients with the broth. Cover and cook on low or high. Garnish with lemon wedges.

Low   4–6 hours
High   2–3 hours

Somerset herrings

I cup soft breadcrumbs
I cup sliced button mushrooms

I apple, cored and chopped
¼ cup finely chopped shallots
3 tablespoons butter, melted
6 fresh herrings, filleted
I teaspoon dried thyme
I¼ cups hard cider

Mix the breadcrumbs, half the mushrooms, apple, shallots and melted butter. Divide the stuffing between the fillets, placing it at the head end. Fold in half. Place the remaining mushrooms in the bottom of the slow-cooking pot and sprinkle with the thyme. Lay the fish in a circle on top of the mushrooms, slightly overlapping them. Pour the cider over fish. Cover and cook on low or high.

Low   3–4 hours
High   1½–2 hours

Bouillabaisse

Bouillabaisse is the traditional Mediterranean fisherman's soup, made from the day's catch. Its flavor is more interesting if a variety of fish is used. Cooked shellfish can be stirred in half-an-hour before serving.

2 lbs. assorted boned fish (cod, haddock, flounder, halibut, red snapper)
2 tablespoons olive oil
I medium-sized onion, chopped
2 small leeks, sliced
I clove garlic, crushed
I can (16oz.) tomatoes, chopped
few sprigs parsley
bay leaf
pinch basil
large pinch saffron powder
salt and pepper
⅔ cup fish broth or water
I tablespoon chopped parsley to garnish

Cut all the boned fish into bite-sized pieces. Heat the oil in a frying pan and fry the onion and leek gently until transparent and softened. Drain well and mix with all the other ingredients, except the chopped parsley, in the slow-cooking pot. Cover and cook on low or high. Remove bay leaf. Sprinkle liberally with chopped parsley, season to taste with salt and pepper and serve with toasted French bread.

Low   6–8 hours
High   3–4 hours

Bouillabaisse (page 26)

VEGETABLES

The recipes in this section cover a variety of vegetables, including some of the more unusual ones.

When you need to economize on the family budget, a vegetable dish can be nutritious and inexpensive. For instance, you use far less meat if it is stuffed with a tasty vegetable mixture; or cabbage—not often a favorite vegetable—made into rolls filled with ground beef is delicious with its tangy Tomato sauce (see the recipe on page 17).

In a slow-cooking pot many vegetables take as long, if not a little longer, to cook than meat, therefore when combining them with a meat dish, e.g., a casserole, they should be cut into small cubes or thin slices. In most instances, the vegetables should be placed toward the bottom of the pot with the meat on top.

Vegetables develop their full flavor with slow-cooking and often the same flavor as that produced with normal cooking will be obtained using reduced quantities. Therefore when adapting your own recipes, begin by halving the quantity of stronger flavored vegetables such as onions, leeks and peppers.

Dried vegetables, such as onions or mixed vegetables, are ideal to use, particularly when you are in a hurry. In most cases the dried vegetables can be mixed in with the other ingredients, but refer to the manufacturers' directions to be sure.

Many frozen vegetables can be added to casseroles to give added flavor and color. To retain their color and texture these should be added toward the end of the cooking time: during the last half-hour if cooking on high, and the last hour if cooking on low. To ensure that the cooking temperature in the pot is not lowered too far, all frozen vegetables should be thawed before being added.

Some root vegetables, particularly potatoes, tend to discolor during long, slow cooking unless they are completely covered by other foods or liquid. For potatoes to serve around a roast, pre-brown them with the meat before placing in the slow-cooking pot; they won't have crisp skins, but like all slowly cooked vegetables they will have a delicious flavor.

Opposite: Artichokes française (page 34)

Celery and ham roulades

8 ribs celery
4 slices processed cheese
4 slices smoked ham
salt and pepper
I can (10½oz.) condensed cream of celery soup
3 tablespoons water

Wash the celery well and cut each rib into two equal-sized pieces. Divide each slice of cheese into four strips and each slice of ham into two halves. Sandwich two pieces of celery with two strips of the cheese as the filling. Wrap the whole sandwich around with a piece of ham, fasten with toothpicks and place in the slow-cooking pot. Season with salt and pepper. Mix the soup and water and pour evenly over the celery. Cover and cook on low or high.

Low   6–8 hours
High   3–4 hours

Sweet and sour red cabbage

I medium-sized red cabbage
I small onion, grated
2 small cooking apples, peeled and thinly sliced
3 tablespoons firmly packed brown sugar
3 tablespoons vinegar
salt and pepper
⅔ cup hot chicken broth or water

Wash, core and finely shred the cabbage. Mix with all the other ingredients, with salt and pepper to taste, in the slow-cooking pot. Cover and cook on low or high. Stir half way through cooking. Serve hot with pork dishes, or cold as a salad ingredient.

Low   6–8 hours
High   3–4 hours

Vegetable casserole

2 onions, chopped
I clove garlic, crushed
3 tablespoons oil

3 zucchini, thinly sliced
2 cups sliced mushrooms
½lb. yellow turnip or rutabaga, diced
I can (11oz.) kernel corn, drained
½ teaspoon dried rosemary

½ teaspoon cardamom
salt and pepper
⅔ cup beef or chicken broth
chopped chives to garnish

In a skillet, fry the onion and garlic in the oil. Place in the slow-cooking pot with the zucchini, mushrooms, turnip, corn, rosemary, cardamom, salt, pepper and broth. Cover and cook on low. Serve sprinkled with chopped chives.

Low   8–10 hours

Cabbage rolls

12 whole cabbage leaves
¾lb. ground chuck
I small onion, grated
I tablespoon chopped parsley
salt and pepper
3 tablespoons firmly packed brown sugar
I can (16oz.) tomatoes

Wash the cabbage leaves carefully, trim to remove some of heavy ribs and blanch in boiling water for I minute. Drain well. Mix together the chuck, onion, parsley and salt and pepper and divide equally between the leaves, placing the filling at the stalk end. Roll up each leaf turning in sides and place closely together in the slow-cooking pot. Sprinkle with the sugar and pour the roughly chopped tomatoes over cabbage. Cover and cook on low or high.

Low   6–8 hours
High   3–4 hours

Sweet and sour celeriac

I celeriac root
I cup chopped cooked ham
I cup drained pineapple chunks
¼ cup syrup drained from pineapple
I tablespoon firmly packed brown sugar
3 tablespoons soy sauce
3 tablespoons olive oil
3 tablespoons cider vinegar
I tablespoon cornstarch mixed with I tablespoon water

Peel, quarter and dice the celeriac. Blanch in boiling salted water for 30 seconds. Place in the slow-cooking pot with the ham and pineapple. Mix the pineapple juice, brown sugar, soy sauce, oil and vinegar and pour over the celeriac. Cover and cook on low or

high. Stir in the cornstarch mixture half-an-hour before cooking is complete.

Low 8–10 hours
High 4–5 hours

Ratatouille

$\frac{1}{4}$ cup butter
I eggplant, diced
2 medium-sized onions, thinly sliced
2 zucchini, sliced
I clove garlic, crushed
salt and pepper
I green pepper, seeded and sliced
2 medium-sized tomatoes, skinned and sliced

Melt half the butter in a separate pan, lightly sauté the eggplant, onions and zucchini, then transfer to the lightly greased slow-cooking pot. Add the garlic, dot with the remaining butter and season with salt and pepper. Add the green pepper and the tomatoes, season with salt and pepper. Cover and cook on low. Stir thoroughly before serving.

Low 8–10 hours

Braised endive

8 Belgian endive
$\frac{1}{4}$ cup butter
$\frac{1}{2}$lb. bacon, chopped
I onion, sliced
salt and pepper
rind and juice of I orange

Wash the endive, remove any damaged outer leaves and scoop out the core at the base. Melt the butter in a frying pan and lightly fry the endive with the bacon and onion. Place in the well greased slow-cooking pot. Season with salt and pepper and add the orange rind and juice. Cover and cook on low or high. Skim excess fat. Serve endive with pot juices.

Low 6–8 hours
High 3–4 hours

Stuffed summer squash

1$\frac{1}{2}$ cups minced cooked meat
$\frac{1}{2}$ small green pepper, chopped

I can (10$\frac{1}{2}$oz.) condensed Scotch Broth *or*
  1$\frac{1}{4}$ cups canned beef gravy
I teaspoon Worcestershire sauce
salt and pepper
4 medium-sized summer squash

Mix together the meat, green pepper, soup or gravy, Worcestershire sauce and season to taste with salt and pepper. Cut squash in half lengthwise and remove center portion with seeds. Fill the halves with the meat mixture. Press 2 halves together and put into the slow cooking pot. Pour $\frac{1}{2}$ cup water around them. Cover and cook on low or high. Serve garnished with broiled tomatoes and chopped parsley and spoon extra hot gravy over each serving, if desired.

Low 6–8 hours
High 3–4 hours

Stuffed green peppers

4 medium-sized green peppers
2 cups cooked long grain rice
$\frac{1}{2}$ cup diced cooked ham or crumbled bacon
$\frac{1}{2}$ cup chopped mushrooms
I small onion, finely chopped
3 tablespoons tomato ketchup
salt and pepper
$\frac{2}{3}$ cup beef broth or water
2 tablespoons butter

Wash the peppers, cut in half and remove seeds. Parboil in water 5 minutes. Drain. Mix together the rice, ham, mushrooms, onion and ketchup and season with salt and pepper. Fill each pepper half with the mixture. Place the peppers in the slow-cooking pot and pour the broth around them. Top each pepper with a small pat of butter. Cover and cook on low or high.

Low 6–8 hours
High 3–4 hours

Artichokes française

2 artichokes
I clove garlic
I cup sliced mushrooms
2 medium-sized tomatoes
I teaspoon fines herbes
salt and pepper
$\frac{2}{3}$ cup white wine

Wash the artichokes well in salted water. Trim the sharp points of the leaves square with scissors and cut off stalk at the base. Cut each one into quarters and

remove the hairy choke. Cook in boiling salted water for 5 minutes. Drain well. Rub the cut clove of garlic around the inside of the slow-cooking pot. Place the mushrooms in the bottom. Skin tomatoes by placing in boiling water 1 minute. Core and quarter the tomatoes, remove the seeds and slice thinly. Place in the slow-cooking pot with the herbs, salt and pepper and white wine. Place the artichoke quarters on top, cover and cook on low or high.

Low   6–8 hours
High   3–4 hours

Fennel and potato

2 heads fennel
1lb. potatoes
1lb. spinach
salt and pepper
juice and rind of 1 lemon
large pinch of dried dill weed
¾ cup (3oz.) grated sharp Cheddar cheese

Trim and thinly slice the fennel. Blanch for 1 minute in boiling salted water. Drain. Peel and slice the potatoes. Wash the spinach well, trim heavy stems. Place half the potatoes in the greased slow-cooking pot, followed by half the spinach and fennel, seasoning each layer well. Sprinkle the grated lemon rind, juice and dill over the fennel. Repeat the layers. Cover and cook on low or high. Spoon vegetables on a heatproof platter. Sprinkle the top with grated cheese and brown under broiler.

Low   8–10 hours
High   4–5 hours

NOTE: If you have a stoneware pot, leave vegetables in pot, sprinkle with cheese and broil as above after removing from base.

Leek and bacon pudding

½lb. bacon in one piece
2 leeks, finely sliced
1 cup (4oz.) grated sharp Cheddar cheese
2 eggs
1¼ cups milk
½ teaspoon dry mustard
black pepper

Cut bacon into small cubes. In a skillet fry bacon very gently without extra fat for 2–3 minutes. Add the leeks and fry until lightly browned. Transfer to the slow-cooking pot with ¾ cup of the cheese. Beat together the eggs, milk, mustard and pepper. Pour over the other ingredients. Cover and cook on low. Spoon carefully onto heatproof serving dish. Sprinkle the top with the remaining cheese and brown under a hot broiler.

Low   2½–3 hours

NOTE: If you have a stoneware pot, leave vegetables in pot. Remove from base, sprinkle with cheese and broil as above.

Boston baked beans

½lb. navy or pea beans
water to cover
1 celery heart, roughly chopped
1 tablespoon soft brown sugar
3 tablespoons molasses
2 teaspoons dry mustard
½lb. bacon in one piece, cut into ½-inch thick slices
black pepper

Wash the beans and put them into the slow-cooking pot with just enough water to cover. Cook on low overnight to let the beans soften. Drain off any excess liquid, leaving the beans still just covered with liquid. Stir in the celery, sugar, molasses and mustard. Lay the bacon on the beans and season with black pepper. Cover and cook on low or high. Spoon the beans and sliced bacon into a serving dish.

Low   8–10 hours
High   4–5 hours

Italian stuffed tomatoes

4 large even-sized tomatoes
1 small onion, finely chopped
1 tablespoon oil
½lb. ground chuck
1 cup soft breadcrumbs
½ teaspoon oregano
salt and pepper

Cut a thin slice from the bottom of each tomato (not the stalk end). Carefully scoop out the seeds with a teaspoon. Strain the juice from the seeds and set aside. Sauté the onion in the oil. Add the chuck and cook for 2 minutes. Stir in breadcrumbs, reserved tomato juice, oregano and salt and pepper. Fill the

tomatoes with the mixture and put the tomato lids on top. Place in the slow-cooking pot with $\frac{1}{4}$ cup water. Cover and cook on low or high.

Low   4–6 hours
High   2–3 hours

Stuffed acorn squash

2 acorn squash
salt and pepper
$\frac{1}{2}$lb. sausage meat
2 hard-cooked eggs, chopped
$\frac{1}{2}$ cup chopped mushrooms
1 tablespoon chopped parsley
$\frac{1}{4}$ teaspoon thyme
1 cup soft breadcrumbs
2 tablespoons butter

Wash and dry the squash. Cut into halves. Scoop out the seeds and sprinkle with salt and pepper. Mix remaining ingredients together (except butter) and fill the squash halves. Dot with butter and place in slow-cooking pot. Dot with butter. Cover and cook on low or high.

Low   6–8 hours
High   3–4 hours

Corn-on-the-cob

1 corn cob per person
1$\frac{1}{4}$ cups water
melted butter
freshly ground black pepper

Remove the outer green leaves and 'silk' from the corn and wash thoroughly. Place in the slow-cooking pot with the water. Cover and cook on low.
Serve with plenty of melted butter and freshly ground black pepper.

Low   6–8 hours

Eggplant florentine

1$\frac{1}{2}$lbs. spinach
2 small eggplants
1 tablespoon butter
2 hard-cooked eggs, sliced
salt and pepper
1$\frac{1}{2}$ cups (6oz.) grated sharp Cheddar cheese

Wash the spinach very thoroughly, trim tough stems and cook in a small amount of boiling salted water for 1 minute. Slice the eggplants, sprinkle with salt and

37

allow to drain for half-an-hour, then rinse and dry. Lightly grease the slow-cooking pot. Place the eggplants in the bottom, top with the eggs, season and sprinkle with I cup of the cheese. Cover with a layer of spinach. Cover and cook on low or high. Spoon on a heatproof serving platter. Sprinkle with the remaining cheese and brown under broiler.

Low 4–5 hours
High 2–2½ hours

NOTE: If you have a stoneware pot, leave vegetables in pot, sprinkle with cheese. Remove from base and broil as above.

Braised celery

2 small bunches celery
I large onion, diced
I large carrot, diced
4 slices bacon, chopped
2 tablespoons butter
salt and pepper
1¼ cups chicken broth

Wash the celery, cut each rib in half and blanch in boiling salted water for I minute. Drain. Fry the onion, carrot and bacon in the butter in a skillet until lightly browned. Put in the bottom of the slow-cooking pot and season with salt and pepper. Place the celery on top, add the broth. Cover and cook on low or high. The celery may be served separately with sauce made from the pot juices thickened with flour or cornstarch.

Low 6–8 hours
High 3–4 hours

Celery and cheese soufflé

I tablespoon butter or margarine
I tablespoon all-purpose flour
⅔ cup milk
I teaspoon dry mustard
salt and pepper
¾ cup (3oz.) grated Cheddar cheese
3 eggs, separated
little butter for greasing
I can (15oz.) coeur de celeri

Melt the butter in a separate pan, stir in the flour and cook for I minute. Remove from heat and gradually stir in the milk. Return to heat and bring to a boil, stirring constantly. Stir in the mustard, salt and

pepper and cheese. Allow to cool slightly then stir in egg yolks. Lightly grease a I-quart soufflé dish or I-quart casserole. Drain the celery and place in the bottom of soufflé dish. Beat egg whites until very stiff and fold into the cheese mixture with rubber scraper. Pour mixture over the celery, spreading evenly. Cover the dish with greased aluminum foil. Place the dish in the slow-cooking pot with I cup water around it. Cover and cook on low or high.

Low 3–4 hours
High 1½–2 hours

Zucchini provençale

3 medium-sized zucchini
3 medium-sized tomatoes
¾ cup (3oz.) grated Cheddar cheese
2 tablespoons butter
salt and pepper
pinch dill seed

Cut the zucchini into ½-inch thick crosswise slices. Skin the tomatoes by placing them in boiling water for I minute, then core and cut them into quarters. Layer the zucchini, tomatoes and cheese in the buttered slow-cooking pot, seasoning each layer with salt and pepper and dill seed and ending with cheese. Cover and cook on low or high. Serve cold as an appetizer or hot with lamb or chicken dishes.

Low 6–8 hours
High 3–4 hours

Stuffed zucchini

3 large zucchini
2 tablespoons lard
½lb. ground chuck
I clove garlic, crushed
I tablespoon tomato paste
2 teaspoons soy sauce
salt and pepper

Cut the zucchini in half lengthwise and scoop out the center (a grapefruit knife is useful for this). Chop the squash removed. Heat the lard in a frying pan and quickly brown the meat and garlic. Stir in the paste, soy sauce and chopped squash and season to taste with salt and pepper. Spoon this mixture back into zucchini shells. Place the zucchini in the slow-cooking pot and carefully add ½ cup water around them. Cover and cook on low or high.

Low 5–6 hours
High 2½–3 hours

POULTRY AND GAME

Chicken continues to be one of the most versatile meats around, as well as still being fairly economical. It lends itself well to slow cooking, as this method will leave it both juicy and succulent and, with the addition of just a few vegetables and herbs, a simple chicken becomes a well-flavored dish.

Fricassée chickens can be substituted in many of the recipes and are often cheaper than the roasting or frying variety. When using fricassée chicken increase the cooking time by at least 2 hours on the low setting or 1 hour on the high setting.

All frozen poultry or game MUST be thoroughly thawed before cooking starts.

Many of the chicken recipes do not require sautéing, therefore these are ideal to choose if you wish to prepare all the ingredients beforehand and store them in the slow-cooking pot overnight. The pot must then be stored in a refrigerator. Before cooking, hot, but not boiling, liquid should be added and cooking started on high for at least 30 minutes before turning to the low setting.

If you have never tried game, now is the time to begin. Slow cooked with a few vegetables and seasonings even the slightly tougher game will be moist and tender. Rabbit is so often overlooked and yet it remains in the bracket of the less expensive meats: try the Rabbit casserole on page 46 and you will be sure to want to use it again.

Opposite Poussin Véronique (page 45)

Roast chicken

2–3lbs. roasting chicken
$\frac{1}{4}$ cup butter
salt and pepper

Wash and dry the chicken. Before cooking, check that the whole chicken is the right size for the pot and that the lid of the slow-cooking pot will fit correctly. Heat the butter in a separate pan and brown the chicken on all sides. Transfer to the lightly greased slow-cooking pot and season with salt and pepper. Cover and cook on high. If you prefer a crisp finish to the chicken, place chicken in another pan and roast at 400°F. for 15 minutes.

High   6–7 hours

NOTE: If you have a stoneware pot, remove pot from base and roast as above.

Fricassée fowl

3–3$\frac{1}{2}$lbs. fricassée fowl
1 onion, thinly sliced
1 carrot, sliced
1 rib celery, chopped
bouquet garni (thyme, parsley, celery leaves)
salt and pepper
1$\frac{1}{4}$ cups boiling water or chicken broth

Cut chicken into serving size pieces. Place the vegetables in the bottom of the slow-cooking pot, add the fowl, bouquet garni, salt, pepper and liquid. Cover and cook on high or high *and* low.
     The broth obtained from cooking this dish can be used as a base for a delicious soup.

High   5–6 hours *or*
High   1 hour *then*
Low   8–10 hours

Chicken in a pot

1 chicken (3lbs.), cut-up
1 onion, sliced
2 carrots, sliced
3 ribs celery, chopped
salt and pepper
$\frac{2}{3}$ cup white wine
$\frac{2}{3}$ cup chicken broth
$\frac{1}{2}$ teaspoon sweet basil

Wash chicken and pat dry. Put the vegetables into the slow-cooking pot and place the chicken on top.

Season with salt and pepper, and add white wine, broth and basil. Cover and cook on low or high. If the chicken is taken straight from the refrigerator and you wish to use the low setting, cook on high 30 minutes, then low 7–9 hours.

Low   8–10 hours
High   4–5 hours

Chicken curry

1 chicken (3lbs.), cut-up
$\frac{1}{4}$ cup lard
1 medium-sized onion, chopped
salt and pepper
$\frac{1}{4}$ cup yellow raisins
2 tablespoons curry powder
1 tablespoon all-purpose flour
$\frac{1}{2}$ cup beef broth
1 tablespoon cornstarch mixed with 1 tablespoon
     water

Wash chicken and pat dry. Heat the lard in a skillet, lightly brown the chicken pieces and fry the onion until transparent. Drain well, transfer to slow-cooking pot and season with salt and pepper. Add the raisins. Stir the curry powder and flour into the fat and juices left in the skillet. Cook for 1 minute, remove from heat and stir in the broth. Pour sauce over the chicken. Cover and cook on low or high. To thicken the sauce stir in the cornstarch mixture half-an-hour before serving. Serve on a bed of rice with curry accompaniments such as sliced green peppers, bananas (peeled, sliced and sprinkled with lemon juice to prevent discoloration), chutney and coconut.

Low   6–8 hours
High   3–4 hours

Chicken cacciatore

1 medium-sized onion, chopped
$\frac{3}{4}$ cup sliced button mushrooms
1 chicken (about 3lbs.), cut-up
salt and pepper
1 teaspoon crushed oregano
$\frac{1}{2}$ teaspoon dried basil
bay leaf
$\frac{2}{3}$ cup chicken broth or dry white wine
3 tablespoons tomato paste
peas and chopped parsley to garnish

Put the onion and mushrooms in the slow-cooking pot. Lay the chicken pieces on top, add the salt, pepper, herbs and broth or wine. Cover and cook on low or high. If the chicken is taken straight from the

refrigerator and you wish to use the low setting, cook on high 30 minutes, then low 7–9 hours. Half-an-hour before serving stir in the tomato paste and baste the chicken with the liquid. Garnish with cooked peas and chopped parsley.

Low   8–10 hours
High   4–5 hours

Chicken casserole

1 medium-sized onion, thinly sliced
1 small green pepper, seeded and thinly sliced
1 can (11oz.) kernel corn, drained
1 chicken (3lbs.), cut-up
1 can (10¾oz.) condensed cream of mushroom soup
salt and pepper

Put the onion, pepper and corn in the slow-cooking pot. Lay the chicken pieces on top. Add the soup and seasoning. Cover and cook on low or high. If the chicken is taken straight from the refrigerator and you wish to use the low setting, cook on high 30 minutes, then low 7–9 hours.

Low   8–10 hours
High   4–5 hours

Chicken and vegetable pie

1 medium-sized onion, sliced
¼lb. button mushrooms
1 chicken (3lbs.), cut into quarters
salt and pepper
few sprigs parsley
bay leaf
sprig fresh thyme
⅔ cup chicken broth
1 can (10¾oz.) condensed cream of mushroom soup
1 package (10oz.) frozen mixed vegetables
pie crust made from 1½ cups all-purpose flour or
    1 package (11oz.) pie crust mix

Put the vegetables and chicken pieces in the slow-cooking pot. Season with salt and pepper, add the herbs and hot broth. Cover and cook on high then low or continuously on high. Cool. Remove chicken, skin and bone. Dice meat. Strain the liquid stirring ½ cup of it into the soup. Stir in cooked vegetables, remaining liquid and frozen mixed vegetables. Stir in chicken. Adjust seasoning with salt and pepper. Pour mixture into a 1½-quart shallow casserole.
    Roll out the pastry to fit the top of casserole, sealing edges. Make a hole in the center to allow steam to escape. Bake at 400°F. for 30–35 minutes.

High   3½–4½ hours or
High   ½ hour then
Low   7–9 hours

NOTE: If you have a stoneware pot, leave food in pot and remove from base. Cover with pie crust and bake as above.

Lemon baked chicken

4 chicken breasts
1 clove garlic
grated rind and juice of 1 lemon
salt and pepper
2 tablespoons butter
1 tablespoon oil
3 tablespoons half-and-half
chopped parsley to garnish

Skin the chicken breasts and make a long but shallow cut into the flesh. Place a sliver of garlic, a good pinch of lemon rind and a little salt and pepper in the opening. Heat the butter and oil in a skillet and quickly brown the chicken pieces all over, placing the cut side down first. Drain and transfer to the slow-cooking pot. Add more salt and pepper and the lemon juice. Cover and cook on low or high. Before serving, stir in the cream and sprinkle with parsley.

Low   6–8 hours
High   3–4 hours

Country chicken

1 chicken (3lbs.), cut-up
2 tablespoons butter or margarine
1 tablespoon oil
3 slices bacon, chopped
1 onion, sliced
4 carrots, sliced
1 cup sliced mushrooms
1 can (16oz.) tomatoes
1 tablespoon chopped parsley
salt and pepper

Wash chicken and pat dry. Heat the butter and oil in a skillet and lightly brown the chicken pieces. Drain and transfer to the slow-cooking pot. Add the bacon and vegetables to the skillet and sauté for 2–3 minutes. Add to the chicken with the tomatoes, parsley and salt and pepper. Stir. Cover and cook on low or high.

Low   7–9 hours
High   3½–4½ hours

Rabbit pie

2 tablespoons lard
1 rabbit, cut into serving-size pieces
4 slices bacon, chopped
$\frac{1}{4}$ lb. small white onions
2 carrots, thinly sliced
salt and pepper
bay leaf
1$\frac{1}{4}$ cups chicken broth or water
1 tablespoon cornstarch mixed with 1 tablespoon
  water
pie crust using 1$\frac{1}{2}$ cups all-purpose flour or 1 package
  (11oz.) pie crust mix

Heat the lard in a skillet. Wash and dry the rabbit
thoroughly. Brown rabbit pieces in the hot lard with
the bacon and onions. Transfer to the slow-cooking
pot with the carrots, salt, pepper, bay leaf and broth.
Cover and cook on low or high. Cool. Bone rabbit,
cut meat into bite-size pieces. Pour liquid from
slow-cooking pot into a saucepan. Stir in cornstarch
mixture to thicken the cooking liquid. Remove the
bay leaf and stir in rabbit pieces. Pour into a 1$\frac{1}{2}$ quart
shallow casserole. Roll out the pie crust to fit the
casserole. Moisten the side edge of the casserole with
water before laying the pie crust over the filling; press
lightly against the sides and make a steam hole in the
center. Bake in an oven at 400°F. for 30–40 minutes
until the pie crust is crisp and golden brown.

Low   6–8 hours
High   3–4 hours

NOTE: If you have a stoneware pot, leave food in pot
and remove from base. Cover with pie crust and bake
as above.

Poussin Véronique

2–4 broilers, depending on size
fresh thyme
2 tablespoons butter
2 ribs celery, chopped
$\frac{1}{4}$ lb. shallots, peeled and chopped
$\frac{2}{3}$ cup white wine
1 cup seedless green grapes
salt and pepper

Sauce
1$\frac{1}{4}$ cups milk
2 tablespoons butter
2 tablespoons all-purpose flour

Wash and dry the broilers. Put a small sprig of
thyme (or a shake of dried thyme) inside the cavity of
each. Heat the butter in a skillet, lightly fry the celery

and shallots, then transfer to the slow-cooking pot.
Lightly brown the broilers, pour the wine over
them in the pan and bring to a boil. Transfer to the
slow-cooking pot, surround with grapes and season
with salt and pepper. Cover and cook on low or high.
When cooked, carefully strain the cooking liquid and
reserve. Add enough milk to make 1$\frac{1}{2}$ cups. Melt the
butter in a saucepan, stir in the flour and cook for a
few minutes. Remove from heat and gradually stir in
the liquid. Return to heat, bring to a boil, stirring
continuously and boil for 2–3 minutes. Season
to taste with salt and pepper and pour over the
broilers.

This dish can also be made with chicken
quarters, allowing the same cooking time.

Low   6–8 hours
High   3–4 hours

Braised hare

1 hare, cut into serving-size pieces
salt and pepper
$\frac{1}{4}$ cup lard
1 medium-sized onion, sliced
4 slices bacon, chopped
1 tablespoon all-purpose flour
1$\frac{1}{4}$ cups cider
3 tablespoons raisins

Wash and dry the hare and sprinkle pieces with salt
and pepper. Heat the lard in a skillet and fry the

onion and bacon until lightly browned. Transfer to the slow-cooking pot. Brown the hare pieces all over and add to the pot. Drain off all but 1 tablespoon of the fat in skillet, stir in the flour and cook for a few minutes. Stir in the cider and raisins. Bring to a boil, stirring well, then pour over the hare. Cover and cook on low or high.

Low   10–12 hours
High 5–6 hours

This recipe can be used equally well for rabbit; reduce cooking time to:

Low   8–10 hours
High 4–5 hours

Rabbit casserole

1 rabbit, cut into serving-size pieces
salt and pepper
2 tablespoons butter
1 medium-sized onion, sliced
2 teaspoons chopped parsley
1 can (16oz.) tomatoes
bay leaf

Season the rabbit with salt and pepper. Heat the butter in a skillet, brown the rabbit pieces, then drain on paper towels. Lightly sauté the onion. Place all the ingredients in the slow-cooking pot. Cover and cook on low or high. Half-an-hour before serving, baste the rabbit with the cooking liquid. Remove bay leaf before serving.

Low   6–8 hours
High 3–4 hours

Rabbit fricassée

1 rabbit, cut into serving-size pieces
salt and pepper
3 slices bacon, chopped
1 large onion, sliced
2-inch piece lemon rind
$\frac{2}{3}$ cup chicken broth
1 tablespoon all-purpose flour mixed with
    1 tablespoon water
chopped parsley and toast triangles to garnish

Wipe the rabbit pieces and season with salt and pepper. Fry the bacon gently in a skillet until the fat runs, add the onion and cook until transparent. Transfer to the slow-cooking pot. Lightly brown the rabbit pieces in the skillet and add to the slow-cooking pot with the lemon rind and broth. Cover and cook

on low or high. To thicken the liquid, stir in the flour mixture half-an-hour before cooking is complete. Garnish with chopped parsley and triangles of toast.

Low   6–8 hours
High 3–4 hours

Rabbit with mustard

1 rabbit, cut into serving-size pieces
$\frac{1}{4}$ cup dry mustard
2 teaspoons all-purpose flour
2 tablespoons lard
1 small onion, thinly sliced
salt and pepper
$1\frac{1}{4}$ cups chicken broth or water
1 teaspoon cornstarch mixed with 1 tablespoon water
2 tablespoons heavy cream (optional)

Wipe the rabbit pieces, making sure that they are as dry as possible. Mix together two tablespoons of the dry mustard and the flour. Coat the rabbit pieces in this mixture. Heat the fat in a skillet, lightly brown the rabbit pieces and fry the onion until transparent. Drain well, transfer to the slow-cooking pot and season with salt and pepper. Add the remaining dry mustard to the juices and fat left in the skillet. Stir in the broth and bring to a boil. Pour over the rabbit. Cover and cook on low or high. Half-an-hour before serving, stir the cornstarch mixture into the cooked ingredients. For special occasions, stir 2 tablespoons heavy cream into sauce before serving.

Low   6–8 hours
High 3–4 hours

Turkey roll

$\frac{1}{4}$ cup sugar
2 tablespoons cornstarch
1 cup fresh cranberries
1 (2–2$\frac{1}{2}$lbs.) turkey roll, thawed
salt and pepper

In a small saucepan, mix sugar and cornstarch and stir in cranberries. Cook and stir until mixture is bubbly and slightly thickened. Place turkey roll in slow-cooking pot. Sprinkle lightly with salt and pepper. Pour sauce over turkey. Cover and cook on low. (Insert meat thermometer in turkey roll the last 2 or 3 hours; cover and cook until temperature reaches 185°F.) Slice turkey; spoon some of the sauce over turkey, serve the rest separately.

Low   8–10 hours or until 185°F. on meat
         thermometer

Turkey in madeira

2 turkey thighs, about 2½–3lbs.
salt and pepper
2 tablespoons butter
¼lb. small white onions
¼lb. button mushrooms
⅔ cup chicken broth
⅔ cup Madeira
I teaspoon lemon juice
2 teaspoons cornstarch mixed with I tablespoon
  water

Skin the turkey if preferred. Dust well with salt and
pepper. Heat the fat in a skillet and brown the turkey
on all sides. Drain and transfer to the slow-cooking
pot. Brown the onions and mushrooms in the skillet
and add to the turkey with the broth, Madeira and
lemon juice. Cover and cook on low or high. Before
serving, stir in the cornstarch mixture to thicken
sauce. For special occasions, mix I egg yolk with ¼ cup
heavy cream to thicken sauce. Stir in just before
serving to prevent curdling.

Low   8–10 hours
High   4–5 hours

Duckling with cherries

I duckling (3½–4lbs.), quartered
salt and pepper
2 tablespoons butter or margarine
I tablespoon cooking oil
I small onion, chopped
I tablespoon all-purpose flour
I can (8oz.) pitted dark sweet cherries
3 tablespoons sherry
I tablespoon firmly packed brown sugar
½ teaspoon ground cinnamon
I beef bouillon cube
I tablespoon cornstarch mixed with I tablespoon
  water
watercress to garnish

Trim the duck of excess fat, prick the flesh with a fork
and season with salt and pepper. Heat the butter and
oil in a skillet and gently sauté the onion until
transparent and the duck until golden brown. Drain
well and transfer to slow-cooking pot. Drain off all but
I tablespoon of the fat from the skillet, stir in flour
and cook for a few minutes. Drain the cherries,

retaining $\frac{1}{2}$ cup of the juice. Mix this with the remaining ingredients, except the cornstarch, and stir into skillet, stirring continuously. Cook until thickened then stir in the cherries and pour sauce over the duck. Cover and cook on low or high. Skim excess fat. Half-an-hour before serving, stir in cornstarch mixture and garnish with watercress.

Low   8–10 hours
High   4–5 hours

Duck à l'orange

1 duckling (3–3$\frac{1}{2}$lbs.)
salt and pepper
$\frac{1}{4}$ cup all-purpose flour
2 tablespoons butter
1 small onion, chopped
$\frac{1}{2}$ cup mushrooms, sliced
1 large navel orange
1$\frac{1}{4}$ cups fresh orange juice
2 teaspoons all-purpose flour mixed with 1 tablespoon
   water
watercress to garnish

Divide the duck into quarters, sprinkle with salt and pepper and coat with flour. In a skillet heat the butter and fry the duck until lightly browned. Transfer to the slow-cooking pot. Lightly sauté the onion and mushrooms in skillet and add to the slow-cooking pot with the grated rind of the orange and the orange juice. Cover and cook on low or high. Half-an-hour before serving, stir in the flour mixture

and baste the duck well with the sauce. Slice skin and white membrane from the orange. Slice orange and arrange slices on the duck portions. Garnish with watercress before serving.

Low   8–10 hours
High   4–5 hours

Rabbit and partridge casserole

1 rabbit, quartered
2 partridges, thawed
2 tablespoons lard
2 large carrots, sliced
1 medium-sized onion, sliced
salt and pepper
1$\frac{1}{4}$ cups beef broth
1 tablespoon cornstarch mixed with 1 tablespoon
   water
1 tablespoon fresh chopped mixed herbs (thyme, sage, oregano) to garnish

Wash and dry the rabbit and partridges. Split the partridges in two along the breast bone. Heat the lard in a skillet and brown the rabbit and partridges evenly. Drain and transfer to the slow-cooking pot. Sauté the carrots and onion in the skillet until lightly browned, then transfer to the pot. Season with salt and pepper and stir in broth. Cover and cook on low or high. Half-an-hour before serving, stir in the cornstarch mixture to thicken sauce. Sprinkle with fresh herbs to garnish. (If fresh herbs are not

available, add a teaspoon of fines herbes at the beginning of cooking.)

Low   8–10 hours
High 4–5 hours

Game hens with grapes

2 large game hens, about 1lb. each
$\frac{1}{4}$ cup butter
6 slices bacon
$\frac{1}{4}$lb. shallots, peeled and chopped
1 cup stemmed blue grapes
$1\frac{1}{4}$ cups hot beef broth
salt and pepper
3 tablespoons sherry
2 teaspoons cornstarch mixed with 1 tablespoon
   water

Wash and dry the game hens. Split each hen into halves. Heat the butter in a skillet and brown the game hens all over. Drain and transfer to the slow-cooking pot. Lightly brown the bacon and shallots in the hot fat. Lay the bacon slices over the breasts of the birds and put the shallots and halved, pitted grapes around them. Pour the broth over game hens and add salt and pepper. Cover and cook on high then low or high continuously. Half-an-hour before serving, pour the sherry over the birds. Stir the cornstarch mixture into the cooking liquid and baste the birds well.

High 1 hour *then*
Low   6–8 hours *or*
High 4–5 hours

Pâté de foie de volaille

$\frac{3}{4}$lb. chicken livers
2 tablespoons Madeira
crumbled bay leaf
1 clove garlic, crushed
3 slices firm white bread soaked in $\frac{1}{2}$ cup milk
$\frac{1}{4}$lb. cooked ham, chopped
$\frac{1}{2}$lb. bulk sausage
3 tablespoons white wine
$\frac{1}{4}$lb. sliced bacon

Wash the chicken livers and cut each liver into 2 pieces. Place in a bowl with the Madeira, bay leaf and garlic. Cover and leave for 2 hours. Squeeze the

bread dry and crumble finely. Mix with the ham, sausage and liver mixture. Add the wine and leave until mixture is soft. Line a 3-cup ovenproof dish with the bacon slices. Fill with the pâté mixture and cover with greased foil. Stand in the slow-cooking pot and add hot water to come halfway up the dish. Cover and cook on low. Leave to cool in the dish. Cover with a fresh piece of foil and place in the refrigerator for several days to mature. Serve with toast.

Low   4–6 hours

Liver and tomato pâté

$\frac{1}{2}$lb. chicken livers
$\frac{1}{4}$ cup butter
1 onion, finely chopped
1 can (10$\frac{3}{4}$oz.) condensed tomato soup
salt and pepper
3 egg yolks

Wash and dry the chicken livers. In a skillet heat the butter and fry the livers and onion until lightly colored. Put the mixture into an electric blender with the soup, salt and pepper and egg yolks or pass it through a wire strainer. Spoon mixture into 4 lightly greased individual ovenproof dishes. Cover each with greased foil and stand in the slow-cooking pot. Add water to come halfway up sides of dishes. Cover and cook on low or high. Cool, and serve with toast.

Low   6–8 hours
High 3–4 hours

Woodman's casserole

4 pigeons
$\frac{2}{3}$ cup dry red wine
bouquet garni (bay leaf, sage, thyme, parsley)
2 tablespoons lard
4 slices bacon
1 large onion, thinly sliced
2 large carrots, thinly sliced
$\frac{1}{2}$ cup sliced mushrooms
salt and pepper

Place the washed pigeons in a shallow dish and pour the wine over them. Add the bouquet garni and marinate for several hours (or overnight) in the refrigerator, turning them at least once. Heat the fat in a skillet. Chop bacon. Add to skillet and fry with the vegetables until all are very lightly colored. Drain well and transfer to the slow-cooking pot. Drain and dry the pigeons and brown them all over in the hot fat in the skillet. Pour the marinating wine over them in the skillet and bring to a boil. Transfer to the

slow-cooking pot, adding the bouquet garni and salt and pepper. Cover and cook on low or high. Serve with boiled potatoes and a green vegetable.

Low 7–9 hours
High 3½–4½ hours

garnish. Cover and start cooking on high then turn to low, or continue cooking on high. Peel and cut orange into segments and use to garnish the completed dish.

High ½ hour *then*
Low 8–10 hours *or*
High 4–5 hours

Braised pheasant

2 tablespoons butter
1 pheasant
6 ribs celery, cut into 1-inch pieces
1 cup sliced mushrooms
grated rind and juice of 1 orange
1 can (10½oz.) condensed consommé
3 tablespoons sherry
salt and pepper
1 navel orange to garnish

Melt the butter in a skillet, brown the pheasant on all sides, draw to one side and lightly sauté the celery and mushrooms. Transfer these to the slow-cooking pot, placing the pheasant on top of the vegetables. Add the remaining ingredients except orange for

Partridge in red wine

¼ cup butter
2 partridges
1 small onion, chopped
½ cup button mushrooms
3 zucchini, sliced
salt and pepper
⅔ cup dry red wine
2 teaspoons all-purpose flour mixed with 1 tablespoon
    water

Heat the butter in a skillet and brown the partridges on all sides. Drain on paper towels. Lightly sauté the onion, mushrooms and zucchini. Transfer to the slow-cooking pot and place the partridges on top. Add salt, pepper and wine. Cover and cook on low or high. Half-an-hour before serving, stir in the flour mixture and adjust the seasoning with salt and pepper. Baste the partridges well with this sauce.

Low 8–10 hours
High 4–5 hours

Winter chicken with dumplings

1 chicken (3lbs.), cut into quarters
2 tablespoons lard
1 medium-sized onion, sliced
1 small yellow turnip or rutabaga, diced
1 small white turnip, diced
2 small leeks, sliced
salt and pepper
1¼ cups chicken broth or water

Dumplings
¼ cup vegetable shortening
1 cup self-rising flour
salt and pepper
large pinch of tarragon (optional)
water to mix

Wash chicken and pat dry. Heat the lard in a skillet and brown the chicken evenly. Drain and transfer to the slow-cooking pot. Lightly sauté all the vegetables, add to the chicken. Season with salt and pepper and add the broth. Cover and cook on low or high. Before making dumplings, turn to high setting. Cut shortening into flour until fine particles. Add salt and pepper, tarragon and enough water to make a firm dough. Beat well. Divide the mixture into 6 equal portions and shape each into ball. Drop the dumplings into the liquid and continue cooking, covered, on high for 30 minutes.

Low 8–10 hours
High 4–5 hours

Braised cider chicken

1 chicken (3lbs.), cut into quarters
bay leaf
pinch of tarragon
salt and pepper
1¼ cups hard cider
2 tablespoons butter
1 medium-sized onion, sliced
3 ribs celery, chopped

2 teaspoons cornstarch mixed with 1 tablespoon water
½ cup heavy cream (optional)

Wash chicken and pat dry. Put in a large bowl with the herbs, salt and pepper and cider and marinate for a few hours or overnight in a refrigerator. Drain and dry the chicken thoroughly. Heat the butter in a skillet and brown the chicken thoroughly with the onion and celery. Transfer the vegetables to the slow-cooking pot, put the chicken pieces on top and pour the marinating liquid over chicken. Cover and cook on low or high. Just before serving, thicken sauce with the cornstarch mixture. For special occasions also stir in ½ cup heavy cream.

Low 7–9 hours
High 3½–4½ hours

Oriental chicken

1 chicken (3lbs.), quartered
salt and pepper
2 tablespoons lard
1 red pepper, seeded and chopped
1 small onion, chopped
1¼ cups beef broth
1 tablespoon firmly packed brown sugar
2 teaspoons soy sauce
½ teaspoon ground ginger
1 cup well drained pineapple chunks
2 teaspoons cornstarch mixed with 1 tablespoon water

Wash chicken and pat dry. Season with salt and pepper. Heat the fat in a skillet and brown the chicken evenly. Drain and transfer to the slow-cooking pot with remaining ingredients except cornstarch. Stir well. Cover and cook on low or high. Before serving stir in cornstarch mixture. Serve with fried rice.

Low 8–10 hours
High 4–5 hours

Fried rice
1 cup long grain rice
3 tablespoons olive oil
1 small onion, chopped
2 teaspoons soy sauce
2 eggs, beaten

Cook the rice in boiling salted water until tender. Drain and rinse with boiling water. Heat the oil in a skillet and cook the onion until it is beginning to brown. Add the rice, stir well, then add the soy sauce and eggs. Continue cooking and stirring until the rice is dry and the egg cooked.

MEAT

Slow cooking makes any meat more tender and really full of flavor. With a slow-cooking pot to cook it in, this means that you can buy the cheaper, usually less tender cuts, and know you can still serve a tasty, nutritious meal. Not only will this help your food budget, but it will give more scope and variety to your everyday cooking.

To enhance the flavor and appearance, most recipes suggest that the meat is pre-browned before going into the slow-cooking pot. This must, of course, be done in a separate pan. This preparation also helps to hasten the heating-through of the meat at the beginning of the cooking period. If pre-browning is eliminated, it is recommended that the recipe is cooked for I hour on the high setting before turning to low. A bouillon cube or a little gravy browning should also be added to give the same color achieved by pre-browning.

During slow cooking, the meat juices and cooking liquid will not evaporate, therefore all the flavor and goodness is retained. This also means that recipes use approximately half the liquid that would normally be required. Thickening of a gravy or sauce should be done at the completion of cooking, using cornstarch or all-purpose flour.

Cooking times for meat dishes are the least critical of all. Many of the dishes quote 8 - 10 hours on low but cooking is so slow that an hour or two longer makes very little difference.

Dumplings add body to any stew or casserole. These can be added half-an-hour before the dish is required; cooked on the high setting, they will be light and fluffy every time.

As the slow-cooking pot heats so slowly, all frozen meats MUST be thoroughly thawed before cooking starts.

It's a good idea, when you can, to cook extra portions of your favorite dish to freeze for future use. It is important that the cooked food is cooled and frozen as quickly as possible. The quickest way is to transfer the food to the storage container, cool it thoroughly by standing the container in cold water, then cover and freeze in the normal way.

Opposite: Chuck roast with vegetables (page 62)

Boiled beef and dumplings

3lbs. corned beef
1 medium-sized onion, sliced
3 medium-sized carrots, sliced
salt and pepper
2½ cups boiling water

Dumplings
1 cup self-rising flour
¼ cup shredded suet or vegetable shortening
salt and pepper
water to mix

Soak the corned beef in water to cover overnight to remove any excess salt. Drain. Put the beef and vegetables into the slow-cooking pot with salt and pepper and boiling water. Cover and cook on high then low, or high continuously. Before making the dumplings, turn the slow-cooking pot setting to high. Mix together the sifted flour, suet (or cut in shortening until particles are very fine) and salt and pepper, with enough water to make a firm dough. Divide the mixture into 6 equal portions and shape each into a ball. Drop the dumplings into the liquid and continue cooking covered on high for 30 minutes.

High   5–6 hours *or*
High   1 hour *then*
Low   8–10 hours or overnight

Steak and kidney pie

1½lbs. round steak
2 lamb's kidneys
3 tablespoons flour mixed with salt and pepper
2 tablespoons lard or vegetable shortening
⅔ cup sherry or beef broth
pinch of thyme
bay leaf
1 cup sliced mushrooms
pie crust made from 1½ cups all-purpose flour
   or 1 package (11oz.) pie crust mix

Cut the steak into 1-inch cubes and the kidneys into small pieces and toss in the seasoned flour. Melt the lard in a skillet and fry the meats until brown. Transfer to the slow-cooking pot with remaining ingredients, except pie crust. Cover and cook on low or high. Season to taste with salt and pepper. Allow the meat mixture to cool slightly. Remove the bay leaf. Pour meat mixture into a shallow 1-quart casserole.
   Roll out the pie crust to fit the top of the casserole. Moisten the side edge of the casserole with

water before laying the pie crust over the filling, press lightly against the sides and make a steam hole in the center. Bake in a 400°F. oven for 30–40 minutes, until the crust is crisp and golden brown.

Low   8–10 hours
High   4–5 hours

NOTE: If you have a stoneware pot, leave food in pot and remove from base. Cover with pie crust and bake as above.

Beef casserole

2lbs. beef chuck, cut into 1-inch cubes
oil or lard for frying
1 onion, chopped
1 cup sliced mushrooms
1¼ cups beef broth or 1 can (10½oz.) condensed beef
   broth
salt and pepper
¼ cup all-purpose flour mixed with ½ cup beef broth

In a skillet fry the beef in the oil until browned and the onion until transparent. Lift out and drain on paper towels. Transfer to the slow-cooking pot, add the mushrooms, broth or soup and salt and pepper. Cover and cook on low or high. To thicken turn to high, stir in the flour mixture half-an-hour before cooking time is complete and correct seasoning with salt and pepper.

Low   8–10 hours
High   4–5 hours

Braised oxtail

2lbs. oxtail, cut into 2-inch pieces
salt and pepper
1 medium-sized onion, sliced
2 tablespoons drippings or vegetable shortening
2–3 large carrots, sliced
bouquet garni (bay leaf, parsley, thyme)
1¼ cups beef broth
¼ cup all-purpose flour mixed with ½ cup beef broth
2 teaspoons redcurrant jelly
⅓ cup red wine

Wipe and trim fat from the oxtail pieces, sprinkle well with salt and pepper. Sauté the onion in the drippings in a skillet for a few minutes until light golden brown, add the oxtail and cook until lightly browned. Drain on paper towels, then transfer to the slow-cooking pot. Add the carrots, bouquet garni and broth. Cover and cook on low or high. Turn to high. Stir in the flour mixture half-an-hour before cooking time is complete. Just before serving stir in redcurrant jelly and wine, and season to taste with salt and pepper. Cover and simmer another 5 minutes.

Low 10–12 hours
High 5–6 hours

Savory ground beef cobbler

1 tablespoon oil
1½lbs. ground beef
1 small onion, chopped
½ cup sliced mushrooms
2 teaspoons curry powder
1 tablespoon all-purpose flour
⅔ cup beef broth
salt and pepper

Topping
2 cups self-rising flour
¼ cup margarine
salt and pepper
about ⅔ cup milk

In a skillet heat the oil and cook the beef until brown and crumbly. Drain well and transfer to the

slow-cooking pot. Lightly sauté the onion and mushrooms in the skillet, then stir in the curry powder, flour, broth, salt and pepper. Pour sauce over ground beef and stir thoroughly. Cover and cook on low or high. Pre-heat oven to 425°F. Pour mixture into a 1½-quart casserole. Mix flour and margarine until margarine particles are very fine. Season with salt and pepper. Stir in enough milk to make a soft dough. Knead a few times, on a floured surface, until a smooth ball. Roll out to ½-inch thickness. Cut with a cookie cutter into 2-inch rounds. Place rounds overlapping on top of filling. Bake for 15–20 minutes or until topping is brown and crisp.

Low 4–6 hours
High 2–3 hours

NOTE: If you have a stoneware pot, leave food in pot and remove from base. Cover with crust and bake as above.

Rich beef casserole

2lbs. beef chuck or round
¼ cup lard or vegetable shortening
1 medium-sized onion, sliced
1 clove garlic, crushed
2 carrots, sliced
2 ribs celery, chopped
1 can (16oz.) tomatoes
⅔ cup red wine
salt and pepper
1 tablespoon all-purpose flour

Cut the beef into 1-inch cubes. Melt the lard in a skillet and brown the beef and onion. Drain on paper towels, then transfer to the slow-cooking pot. Add remaining ingredients, except flour mixture. Cover and cook on low or high. To thicken the sauce turn to high and stir in the flour and water mixture half-an-hour before cooking time is complete.

Low 8–10 hours
High 4–5 hours

Pot roast of beef

3lbs. fresh beef brisket
2 tablespoons lard or drippings
1 onion, sliced
2 carrots, sliced
2 ribs celery, chopped
salt and pepper
⅔ cup boiling beef broth

Trim the brisket of excess fat and tie into shape that

will fit into pot with string. In a separate pan heat the lard, brown the brisket all over, drain well and transfer to the slow-cooking pot. Lightly sauté the vegetables and arrange around the meat. Season and add the boiling broth. Cover and cook on high then low or high continuously.

High 5–6 hours *or*
High 1 hour *then*
Low 8–10 hours

Family shepherd's pie

2 tablespoons lard or vegetable shortening
1 medium-sized onion, chopped
2 carrots, grated
½ cup chopped mushrooms
1½ lbs. ground beef
3 tablespoons all-purpose flour
salt and pepper
⅔ cup beef broth
4 cups seasoned mashed potato
2 tablespoons butter

Melt the lard in a skillet and lightly sauté the onion, carrot and mushrooms. Transfer to the slow-cooking pot. Brown the beef in the skillet and stir in the flour. Transfer the beef to the pot, stir well, add salt and pepper and broth. Cover and cook on low or high. Pour meat mixture into a 1-quart shallow casserole. Cover with mashed potatoes. Dot with butter. Bake at 400°F. for 10–15 minutes or until top is lightly browned.

Low 4–6 hours
High 2–3 hours

NOTE: If you have a stoneware pot, leave food in pot and remove from base. Cover with potatoes and bake as above.

Roasting meat

The roast must be of a suitable size and shape to allow the slow-cooking pot lid to fit tightly during cooking and should not weigh more than 3 pounds.

Suitable roasts include:
Shoulder or ½ leg of lamb.
Cooking time high   5–6 hours.
Shoulder of pork.
Cooking time high   6 hours.
Beef top round.
Cooking time high   4–5 hours.

Before cooking season the roast and brown on all

sides in a skillet. Drain and transfer to the slow-cooking pot. Cook as indicated above.

The meat juices collected in the slow-cooking pot during cooking may be used to make a delicious gravy. Skim excess fat before using juices.

If you prefer a crisp finish to the roast, or if you wish to crisp crackling on pork, transfer the roast to a pan and roast in a hot oven for the last half-hour of given cooking time.

Beef 'n' bean casserole

1½ lbs. ground beef
1 small onion, finely chopped
1 can (8oz.) baked beans
1 can (16oz.) tomatoes
1¼ cups hot beef broth
1 cup pasta wheels, whirls or small shells
½ teaspoon fines herbes
1 teaspoon chili powder
2 teaspoons Worcestershire sauce
salt and pepper
chopped parsley to garnish

Put all the ingredients in the slow-cooking pot and stir very thoroughly. Cover and cook on low or high. An occasional stir during cooking will prevent the pasta from sticking together. Skim excess fat. Garnish with chopped parsley.

Low 6–8 hours
High 3–4 hours

Beef risotto

2 tablespoons oil
1 small onion, chopped
1 small green pepper, seeded and chopped
1 lb. ground beef
½ cup chopped mushrooms
1 cup pre-cooked long grain rice
2 cups beef broth
salt and pepper
grated Parmesan cheese
chopped parsley to garnish

Heat the oil in a skillet and lightly sauté the onion and green pepper. Transfer to the slow-cooking pot. Brown the beef, drain excess fat and add this with remaining ingredients to the pot, adding salt and pepper to taste. Stir thoroughly. Cover and cook on low or high. To serve, sprinkle with grated Parmesan cheese and chopped parsley.

Low 6–8 hours
High 3–4 hours

Farmer's beef stew with herby dumplings

$1\frac{1}{2}$lbs. boneless beef chuck
2 tablespoons lard or vegetable shortening
salt and pepper
I onion, sliced
2 carrots, sliced
2 ribs celery, chopped
$\frac{1}{4}$lb. button mushrooms
4 tomatoes, skinned and quartered
$\frac{2}{3}$ cup beef broth
3 tablespoons tomato paste

Dumplings
I cup self-rising flour
$\frac{1}{4}$ cup shredded suet or vegetable shortening
salt and pepper
$\frac{1}{2}$ teaspoon fines herbes
water to mix

Cut the beef into I-inch cubes. Heat the lard in a skillet and brown the beef. Place half the beef on the bottom of the slow-cooking pot, season with salt and pepper, add the vegetables, then the remaining meat and season again with salt and pepper. Mix together the broth and tomato paste and pour over the other ingredients. Cover and cook on low or high.

Before making the dumplings, turn the slow-cooking pot to high and stir the beef and vegetables. Mix together the flour, suet (or vegetable shortening cut into flour until small particles), salt, pepper and herbs with enough water to make a firm dough. Divide the mixture into 6 equal portions and shape each into a ball. Drop into the liquid and cover and continue cooking on high for 30 minutes.

Low   8–10 hours
High   4–5 hours

Carbonnade of beef

$1\frac{1}{2}$lbs. beef chuck
2 tablespoons lard or vegetable shortening
I medium-sized onion, sliced
I clove garlic, crushed
I tablespoon all-purpose flour
$1\frac{1}{4}$ cups ale or beer
I teaspoon vinegar
salt and pepper
thick slices of French bread spread thickly with
    French mustard

Cut the beef into I-inch cubes. Heat the lard in a skillet and brown the beef and onion. Drain and transfer to slow-cooking pot with the garlic. Stir the

flour into the fat and juices left in skillet, then gradually stir in the ale, vinegar, salt and pepper to taste. Pour sauce over beef. Cover and cook on low or high. Half-an-hour before serving, place the bread, mustard side up, on top of the meat.

Low   8–10 hours
High   4–5 hours

Meatballs in tomato sauce

$1\frac{1}{2}$lbs. ground beef
I small onion, finely chopped
I teaspoon fines herbes
salt and pepper
I egg, beaten
2 tablespoons lard or vegetable shortening
I can (16oz.) tomatoes
$\frac{2}{3}$ cup beef broth
I tablespoon all-purpose flour or cornstarch mixed
    with 2 tablespoons water
chopped parsley to garnish

In a large bowl mix beef, onion, herbs, salt and pepper. Mix with the egg. Divide into 12 equal pieces and form into balls. Roll balls in flour. Heat the fat in a skillet and quickly brown the meatballs all over. Drain well and transfer to slow-cooking pot with the tomatoes and broth. Cover and cook on low or high. To thicken sauce, set on high, stir in the flour or cornstarch mixture half-an-hour before serving. Garnish with chopped parsley.

Low   4–6 hours
High   2–3 hours

Beef roulades

$1\frac{1}{2}$lbs. round steak
I cup herb stuffing mix prepared according to
    package directions
2 tablespoons lard or vegetable shortening
I small onion, chopped
I small green pepper, seeded and sliced
salt and pepper
*$\frac{2}{3}$ cup beef broth
I tablespoon all-purpose flour mixed with
    2 tablespoons water

Cut the round steak in strips about 3×4 inches. Beat each strip with a rolling pin or mallet until it is quite thin. Spread stuffing on each piece, roll up and tie with fine string. Melt the lard in a skillet and brown the beef roulades and onion. Drain well and transfer

to the slow-cooking pot with green pepper, salt, pepper and broth. Cover and cook on low or high. To thicken the gravy, stir in the flour mixture half-an-hour before cooking time is complete. Remove the string before serving.

*Increase to 1¼ cups when cooking on high.

Low   8–10 hours
High   4–5 hours

Continental meat loaf

1lb. ground beef
1 small onion, finely chopped
1 clove garlic, crushed
1 tablespoon chopped parsley
1 cup soft white breadcrumbs
1 can (16oz.) tomatoes, drained and chopped
salt and pepper to taste
1 egg, beaten

In a large mixing bowl, mix all the ingredients thoroughly. Transfer to a lightly greased 1-lb loaf pan

or other suitable container. Press down well and cover with greased aluminum foil. Stand the container in the slow-cooking pot and pour 1 cup cold water around it. Cover and cook on low or high. Serve hot with potatoes and a green vegetable or cold with salad.

Low   6–8 hours
High   3–4 hours

Cowboy casserole

2 tablespoons lard or vegetable shortening
2lbs. beef or pork sausages (if using herb-flavored sausages, omit herbs below)
1 small onion, finely chopped
1 can (16oz.) tomatoes
1 can (16oz.) baked beans
1 teaspoon thyme or sage
salt and pepper
1 teaspoon cornstarch mixed with 1 tablespoon water

Heat the lard in a skillet and very quickly brown the sausages. Drain well and transfer to the slow-cooking pot with remaining ingredients except cornstarch mixture. Cover and cook on low or high. Skim excess fat. To thicken the sauce, stir in the cornstarch mixture half-an-hour before serving.

Low   4–6 hours
High   2–3 hours

Red bean braise

2 tablespoons lard or vegetable shortening
2 carrots, sliced
1 onion, sliced
1½lbs. boneless chuck steak, cut into serving-size
    pieces
salt and pepper
pinch of fines herbes
½ cup red or pinto beans soaked overnight in cold
    water
⅔ cup beef broth
⅔ cup red wine
1 tablespoon all-purpose flour mixed with
    2 tablespoons water

Heat the lard in a skillet and sauté the carrots and onion until lightly browned. Transfer to the slow-cooking pot. Season beef with salt and pepper and brown on both sides. Add to the vegetables with the herbs, drained beans, broth and wine. (All broth can be used if preferred.) Cover and cook on low or high. Half-an-hour before serving, stir the flour mixture into the gravy to thicken.
     This is a rich-flavored dish and boiled or mashed potatoes are a good accompaniment.

Low   8–10 hours
High   4–5 hours

Top round braise

2lbs. beef top round
salt and pepper
large pinch of fines herbes
2 tablespoons lard or vegetable shortening
4 carrots, sliced
2 large onions, sliced
1¼ cups ale or beer
1 tablespoon cornstarch mixed with 1 tablespoon
    water

Season the beef and rub herbs over the surface. Heat the lard in a skillet and brown the beef on all sides. Drain and transfer to the slow-cooking pot. Sauté the carrots and one of the onions in the skillet and place around the meat. Pour the ale over the beef. Cover and cook on high then low or continuously on high. When cooked, remove the beef and cut into thick slices. Stir the cornstarch mixture into the cooking

liquid to thicken. Return the beef to the pot and garnish with fried onion rings.

High   1 hour *then*
Low   8–10 hours *or*
High   5–6 hours

Sausage and vegetable casserole

2–3 white turnips, peeled and diced
2 medium-sized potatoes, peeled and diced
salt and pepper
2 teaspoons chopped parsley
⅔ cup beef broth or water
2oz. tomato paste
3 tomatoes, thickly sliced
2 tablespoons lard or vegetable shortening
1lb. beef or pork sausages

Place the turnips and potatoes in the slow-cooking pot, covering the bottom evenly. Season with salt and pepper. Add the parsley, broth, tomato paste, then a layer of tomatoes. Heat the lard in a skillet and quickly brown the sausages. Drain and lay on top of other ingredients. Season with salt and pepper. Cover and cook on low or high.

Low   4–6 hours
High   2–3 hours

Lasagne

6oz. lasagne noodles
2 tablespoons lard or vegetable shortening
1 small onion, chopped
½ cup chopped mushrooms
1lb. ground beef
1 tablespoon all-purpose flour
3 tablespoons tomato paste
salt and pepper
butter for greasing
1¼ cups white sauce (made with 2 tablespoons
    butter, 2 tablespoons all-purpose flour and
    1¼ cups milk, salt and pepper)
grated Parmesan cheese

Cook the lasagne in briskly boiling salted water for 10 minutes. Drain and rinse with cold water. Heat the lard in a skillet and lightly sauté the onion and mushrooms. Draw to one side and brown the beef. Skim excess fat. Stir in the flour, tomato paste, salt and pepper. Put about half the lasagne noodles on the bottom of the lightly greased slow-cooking pot (trim the noodles to fit into the pot), add half the beef

mixture then half the white sauce and a little Parmesan cheese. Repeat the layers. Cover and cook on low or high. Before serving, sprinkle with Parmesan cheese.

Low   4–6 hours
High   2–3 hours

Chuck roast with vegetables

1 beef chuck roast (3lbs.)
1 teaspoon monosodium glutamate
1 teaspoon salt
$\frac{1}{4}$ teaspoon pepper
2 onions, cut into quarters
4 carrots, cut into quarters
1 rib celery, cut into eight chunks
1 bay leaf
2 tablespoons vinegar
5 cups water
1 small green cabbage, cut into wedges

Sauce
3 tablespoons butter or margarine
1 tablespoon instant minced onion
2 tablespoons all-purpose flour
$1\frac{1}{2}$ cups reserved beef broth
2 tablespoons prepared horseradish
$\frac{1}{2}$ teaspoon salt

Sprinkle meat with seasonings. Place onions, carrots

and celery in slow-cooking pot. Top with meat. Add bay leaf, vinegar and water. Cover pot and cook on low. Remove meat. Skim excess fat from pan juices. Turn to high. Add cabbage wedges. Cover and cook on high for 15 to 20 minutes or until cabbage is done. Meanwhile melt butter in saucepan. Stir in instant onion and flour. Drain $1\frac{1}{2}$ cups broth out of slow-cooking pot. Stir broth, horseradish and salt into saucepan. Cook over low heat stirring constantly, until thickened and smooth. Serve with the roast.

Low   5–7 hours, *then* raise to
High   20 minutes

Cholent

1 cup fresh or frozen and thawed large lima beans
2 medium-sized potatoes, peeled and sliced
1 onion, diced
2lbs. fresh beef brisket, rolled and tied
salt and pepper
1 cup self-rising flour
2 tablespoons vegetable shortening
1 tablespoon chopped parsley
1 potato, grated
1 tablespoon grated onion
about $\frac{1}{3}$ cup water
$2\frac{1}{2}$ cups hot beef broth

Place lima beans in the slow-cooking pot, followed by a layer of sliced potato and finally the diced onion. Make a well in the center and stand the brisket in it. Season with salt and pepper. Mix flour and shortening until particles are very fine. Stir in parsley, grated potato and onion. Bind with water to form a soft but not sticky dough. Form this into 2 rolls and place on either side of the meat. Pour the hot broth over brisket. Cover and cook on high then low, or continuously on high.

High   1 hour *then*
Low   8–10 hours *or*
High   5–6 hours

Navarin of lamb

2 breasts of lamb
$\frac{1}{4}$ cup all-purpose flour mixed with salt and pepper
2 tablespoons lard or vegetable shortening
1 clove garlic, crushed
1 can (8oz.) whole carrots, drained
1 can (16oz.) tomatoes
1 teaspoon fines herbes
salt and pepper

Cut the lamb into portion-size pieces (or ask your

butcher to do this for you). Coat with flour mixture and brown quickly in the lard in a skillet. Drain well and transfer to the slow-cooking pot with remaining ingredients, adding salt and pepper to taste. Cover and cook on low or high.

Low   8–10 hours
High   4–5 hours

Tomato brady

2lbs. neck of lamb
1½lbs. tomatoes, skinned and quartered
½lb. yellow onions, thinly sliced (about 3 large)
salt and pepper

Cut the lamb into chops and trim off some of the fat. Place half the tomatoes in the bottom of the slow-cooking pot, followed by all the onions. Put the

chops on top, and finish with a layer of tomatoes. Season each layer with salt and pepper. Cover and cook on low or high.

Low   9–11 hours
High   4½–5½ hours

Farmhouse lamb

2 tablespoons lard or vegetable shortening
2 breasts of lamb, stuffed and rolled (about 1½lbs. each)
½lb. whole small onions, or 2 large onions, quartered
1 tablespoon Worcestershire sauce
⅔ cup beef broth
salt and pepper
1 package (10oz.) frozen mixed vegetables, thawed

Heat the lard in a skillet and brown the lamb all over.

Add the onions and cook until lightly browned. Transfer the lamb and onions to the slow-cooking pot with the Worcestershire sauce, broth, salt and pepper. Cover and cook on low or high. Half-an-hour before serving, spoon the mixed vegetables around the lamb.

Low   10–12 hours
High 5–6 hours

Summer lamb casserole

8 shoulder lamb chops
2 tablespoons lard or vegetable shortening
1lb. small even-sized new potatoes, scraped
½lb. baby carrots, scraped
sprig rosemary
salt and pepper
⅔ cup beef broth, lamb broth or water

Trim the chops of any excess fat. Heat the lard in a skillet and brown the chops on both sides. Place the vegetables in the slow-cooking pot, add the chops, rosemary, salt, pepper and broth. Cover and cook on low or high. If a thicker gravy is preferred, stir in 2 teaspoons flour mixed with 2 tablespoons water half-an-hour before serving.

Low   8–10 hours
High 4–5 hours

Mutton stew

4–6 mutton chops or shoulder lamb chops
salt and pepper
1 large onion, chopped
2 carrots, diced
1 small yellow turnip, diced
2 cups sliced celery or diced rutabaga
¼ cup pearl barley
1 teaspoon chopped parsley
1¼ cups hot water or chicken broth

Trim excess fat from chops and season well with salt and pepper. Place the vegetables on the bottom of the slow-cooking pot. Add the pearl barley, a little more salt and pepper then the lamb, parsley and hot broth. Cover and cook on high then low, or high continuously.

Dumplings go well with this dish: See recipe under Boiled beef and dumplings, page 54.

High 1 hour *then*
Low   8–10 hours *or*
High 5–6 hours

Irish stew

2½lbs. neck of lamb
2 large onions, sliced
2lbs. potatoes, peeled and sliced
4–6 carrots, sliced
salt and pepper
1¼ cups boiling water or chicken or lamb broth
chopped parsley to garnish

Cut the neck of lamb into chops, trim off some of the fat. Mix the onions, potatoes and carrots and put into the slow-cooking pot. Add the chops and salt and pepper, then add the liquid. Cover and cook on low or high. If lamb is taken straight from the refrigerator and you wish to use the low setting, cook on high for 30 minutes then low for 8–10 hours. Place the lamb and vegetables on a deep serving dish. Skim excess fat from liquid and pour liquid into a saucepan. Boil the liquid rapidly in saucepan until half its volume, then pour sauce over the lamb. Garnish with plenty of chopped parsley.

Low   8–10 hours
High 4–5 hours

Lamb provençale

8 shoulder lamb chops
salt and pepper
2 tablespoons lard or vegetable shortening
8 white onions, peeled and left whole
1 clove garlic, crushed
¼lb. button mushrooms, trimmed
1 can (16oz.) tomatoes
1 tablespoon chopped parsley
1 teaspoon cornstarch mixed with 1 tablespoon water

Sprinkle the chops with salt and pepper. Heat the lard in a skillet and brown the chops on both sides. Transfer to the slow-cooking pot. Lightly brown the onions, garlic and mushrooms. Add to the lamb with the tomatoes and parsley. Cover and cook on low or high. To thicken sauce, stir cornstarch mixture into the pot half-an-hour before serving.

Low   8–10 hours
High 4–5 hours

Stuffed lambs' hearts

6 lambs' hearts
2 cups prepared parsley and thyme stuffing
¼ cup all-purpose flour
salt and pepper

2 tablespoons lard or vegetable shortening
I medium-sized onion, sliced
2 carrots, sliced
2 ribs celery, chopped
1¼ cups beef broth
I tablespoon flour mixed with 2 tablespoons water

Wash the hearts very thoroughly. Trim away any fat, tubes or gristle. Dry on paper towels. Fill with the stuffing and sew up the opening. Coat with flour mixed with salt and pepper. Heat the lard in a skillet and lightly sauté the onion, carrot and celery. Transfer to the slow-cooking pot. Brown the hearts in the hot lard, place on top of the vegetables, add the broth and seasoning. Cover and cook on low or high. To thicken the gravy, stir in the flour mixture half-an-hour before cooking time is complete.

Low   8–10 hours
High   4–5 hours

Lamb and zucchini roll

2 breasts of lamb (ask the butcher to bone them, but
    leave them unrolled)
2 zucchini, thinly sliced
½ cup sliced mushrooms
salt and pepper
2 tablespoons lard or vegetable shortening
⅔ cup beef broth

Cover each breast of lamb with the zucchini and mushrooms. Season with salt and pepper. Roll up each one carefully and as tightly as possible from the thinnest end and tie with string. In a skillet heat the lard and brown the lamb well on all sides. Drain well, transfer to the slow-cooking pot and add the broth. Cover and cook on low or high. Small cubes of potato can be browned in the hot lard with the lamb and cooked around the lamb or, for speed, add drained canned new potatoes half-an-hour before serving.

Low   8–10 hours
High   4–5 hours

Curried lamb

2lbs. boneless lamb, cubed
3 tablespoons oil
¼ cup all-purpose flour
3 tablespoons curry powder (to taste)
1¼ cups beef broth
⅓ cup yellow raisins
2 ribs celery, chopped

3 tablespoons chutney
salt and pepper

Brown the lamb in the oil in a skillet, drain well and transfer to the slow-cooking pot. Stir flour and curry powder into the skillet, stirring until all the drippings are absorbed, remove from heat and stir in the broth. Add to the slow-cooking pot with remaining ingredients and stir thoroughly. Cover and cook on low or high. Season to taste with salt and pepper.

Low   8–10 hours
High   4–5 hours

Braised orange lamb

2 cups soft white breadcrumbs
¼ cup raisins
¼ cup shredded suet or margarine
large pinch of marjoram
salt and pepper
2 large oranges
I egg, beaten
3lbs. shoulder of lamb, boned
2 tablespoons lard or vegetable shortening
⅔ cup beef broth
3 tablespoons red wine
3 tablespoons redcurrant jelly

Mix the breadcrumbs, raisins, suet, marjoram, seasoning and grated orange rinds. Stir in beaten egg.

Spread evenly over the lamb, roll up and tie at
intervals with string. Season with salt and pepper.
Heat the lard in a skillet and brown the lamb all over.
Remove all white membranes from oranges, slice
thickly and arrange on the bottom of the
slow-cooking pot. Place the drained lamb on top and
pour broth and wine over lamb. Cover and cook on
high then low or high continuously. Just before
serving, stir the redcurrant jelly into the cooking
liquid and use to baste the lamb. Cut into slices to
serve.

High 5–6 hours *or*
High 1 hour *then*
Low   8–10 hours

Welsh lamb casserole

4 shoulder lamb chops
3 large leeks
2 tablespoons lard or vegetable shortening
salt and pepper
3 tablespoons water
large pinch of marjoram
2 teaspoons cornstarch mixed with 2 tablespoons
    water

Trim excess fat from chops. Remove tops from leeks,
cut in half then split halves. Wash thoroughly to
remove all dirt, dry well. Heat the lard in a skillet and
lightly fry the leeks, handling them carefully to keep
them in shape. Transfer to the slow-cooking pot,
season with salt and pepper, then add the water.
Brown the chops on both sides in a skillet and arrange
on top of the leeks, adding the marjoram, salt and
pepper. Cover and cook on low or high. Half-an-hour
before serving, stir in the cornstarch mixture to
thicken the gravy.

Low   7–9 hours
High 3½–4½ hours

Lamb chops with mustard and horseradish

2 tablespoons lard or vegetable shortening
6 shoulder lamb chops
1 teaspoon prepared mustard
½ teaspoon paprika
3 tablespoons horseradish sauce
⅔ cup beef broth
salt and pepper
1 tablespoon all-purpose flour mixed with

2 tablespoons water
1 package (10oz.) frozen peas, thawed

Melt the lard in a skillet and brown the chops on both
sides. Drain on paper towels. Spread the chops
lightly with mustard on both sides. Transfer to the
slow-cooking pot. Mix together remaining ingredients,
except flour and peas, and pour over the chops. Cover
and cook on low or high. Half-an-hour before cooking
time is complete, stir in the flour mixture and peas.

Low   6–8 hours
High 3–4 hours

Lambs' tongues in piquant sauce

6 lambs' tongues
1 small onion, finely chopped
1 small green pepper, seeded and finely chopped
3 tablespoons vinegar
3 tablespoons firmly packed brown sugar
1 tablespoon tomato paste
⅔ cup beef broth
salt and pepper
1 tablespoon flour mixed with 2 tablespoons water

Wash and trim the tongues, if necessary. Place in the
slow-cooking pot with all the other ingredients,
except the flour. Cover and cook on high then low, or
high continuously. Half-an-hour before serving, stir in
the flour mixture and season with salt and pepper.

High ½ hour *then*
Low   8–10 hours *or*
High 4–5 hours

Pork tenderloin in sherry

2 pork tenderloin slices, halved
2 tablespoons butter
1 clove garlic, crushed
1 cup sliced mushrooms
2 teaspoons paprika
⅔ cup sherry
2 teaspoons flour mixed with 2 tablespoons water
⅔ cup light cream

Remove fat from tenderloin. In a skillet heat the
butter and fry the pork until lightly browned all
over. Drain well on paper towels, transfer to the
slow-cooking pot and add the garlic and mushrooms.
Add paprika to the juices in the skillet and stir in the

Below: Barbecued pork

sherry. Pour sauce over the pork. Cover and cook on low or high. Half-an-hour before serving, stir in flour mixture. Just before serving, pour the cream over the pork.

Low   8–10 hours
High 4–5 hours

Barbecued pork

4 pork chops
salt and pepper
2 tablespoons lard or vegetable shortening
1 medium-sized onion, chopped
1 tablespoon tomato paste
$\frac{1}{4}$ cup cider vinegar
3 tablespoons firmly packed brown sugar
1 teaspoon dry mustard
2 teaspoons Worcestershire sauce
$\frac{2}{3}$ cup beef broth
1 tablespoon flour mixed with 3 tablespoons water
4 pineapple rings

Sprinkle the chops with salt and pepper. Heat the lard in a skillet and brown the chops on both sides. Drain and transfer to the slow-cooking pot. Lightly fry the onion and add to the chops. Mix together the tomato paste, vinegar, brown sugar, mustard, Worcestershire sauce and broth. Pour mixture over the chops. Cover and cook on low or high. Half-an-hour before serving, skim excess fat from pan juices.

Stir in the flour mixture. Place a pineapple ring on each chop, baste with the sauce and continue cooking.

Low   6–8 hours
High 3–4 hours

Braised pork chops

4 loin pork chops
salt and pepper
3 tablespoons all-purpose flour
2 tablespoons butter
1 large onion, chopped
2 large ribs celery, chopped
3 tomatoes, skinned and chopped or 1 can (16oz.)
2 teaspoons sugar
1 teaspoon Worcestershire sauce
4 medium-sized potatoes, peeled and sliced

Sprinkle chops with salt and pepper. Coat the chops with flour and fry briskly in the butter in a skillet. Drain on paper towels. Add the onion to the skillet and fry gently until light golden brown. Add the celery, tomatoes, sugar and Worcestershire sauce and cook gently 2–3 minutes, stirring well. Lay the potato slices on the bottom of the slow-cooking pot, pour over the mixture from the skillet and arrange the chops on top. Cover and cook on low or high. Correct seasoning with salt and pepper just before serving.

Low   8–10 hours
High 4–5 hours

Curried pork with apricots

$1\frac{1}{2}$lbs. lean boneless pork
2 tablespoons lard or vegetable shortening
1 medium-sized onion, chopped
3 tablespoons curry powder (to taste)
1 tablespoon all-purpose flour
$1\frac{1}{4}$ cups pork or chicken broth or water
$\frac{1}{2}$ cup dried apricots (soak overnight before use)
1 tablespoon chutney
1 tablespoon lemon juice
salt to taste
flaked coconut to garnish

Cut the pork into bite-sized cubes. Heat the lard in a skillet, brown the pork and lightly brown the onion. Drain well on paper towels and transfer to the slow-cooking pot. Add the curry powder and flour to the juices in the skillet, then gradually add the broth, stirring all the time. Bring to a boil then pour over the pork and onion. Add remaining ingredients and stir well. Cover and cook on low or high. Stir well before serving and sprinkle with flaked coconut.

Low   8–10 hours
High   4–5 hours

Pork chops with orange

1 clove garlic
2 teaspoons chopped parsley
2 teaspoons ground fennel
salt and pepper
4 pork chops
3 tablespoons oil
$\frac{2}{3}$ cup fresh orange juice
$\frac{1}{4}$ cup white wine
2 teaspoons cornstarch mixed with 2 tablespoons
   water
1 navel orange
watercress to garnish

Rub the garlic, herbs, salt and pepper into the chops. Heat the oil in a skillet and brown the chops on both sides. Transfer to the slow-cooking pot and add the orange juice and wine. Cover and cook on low or high. Half-an-hour before serving, stir in the cornstarch mixture. Slice the skin and white membrane from the orange and cut into 4 thick slices. Place one slice on each chop and baste with sauce. Serve on a bed of noodles and garnish with watercress.

Low   6–8 hours
High   3–4 hours

Pork chops in cider

2 tablespoons oil
6 loin pork chops
1 small onion, thinly sliced
1 cup sliced mushrooms
salt and pepper
1$\frac{1}{4}$ cups hard cider
1 tablespoon flour mixed with 3 tablespoons water

Heat the oil in a skillet and brown the chops on both sides. Drain on paper towels. Lightly fry the onion in skillet and transfer to the slow-cooking pot with the mushrooms, laying the chops on top. Season with salt and pepper and add the cider. Cover and cook on low or high. Half-an-hour before cooking is complete, stir in the flour mixture to thicken the sauce.

Low   6–8 hours
High   3–4 hours

Hungarian pork

1$\frac{1}{2}$lbs. boneless pork
2 tablespoons lard or vegetable shortening
1 large onion, chopped
1 clove garlic, finely chopped
1 tablespoon paprika
$\frac{1}{2}$ teaspoon caraway seeds
$\frac{1}{2}$ teaspoon cayenne
salt and pepper
large pinch thyme
large pinch marjoram
$\frac{1}{4}$lb. button mushrooms
2 red peppers, seeded and sliced
$\frac{2}{3}$ cup chicken or pork broth
2 teaspoons cornstarch mixed with 2 tablespoons
   water
$\frac{2}{3}$ cup sour cream
chopped parsley to garnish

Cut the pork into 1-inch cubes. Heat the lard in a skillet and lightly brown the pork, onion and garlic. Stir in all the seasonings and herbs. Place the mushrooms and red pepper in the bottom of the slow-cooking pot and add the pork mixture and broth. Cover and cook on low or high. Half-an-hour before serving, stir in the cornstarch mixture. Just before serving, pour in the sour cream and garnish with parsley.

Low   6–8 hours
High   3–4 hours

Pork casserole

1½lbs. lean boneless pork
6 tablespoons honey
⅓ cup cider vinegar
1¼ cups pork broth or chicken broth
¼ cup sherry
3 tablespoons soy sauce
1 clove garlic, crushed
¼ cup all-purpose flour
½ cup canned kernel corn with juice
salt and pepper

Trim any excess fat from meat, cut into cubes and put in the slow-cooking pot. Mix together the honey, vinegar, broth, sherry, soy sauce and garlic and pour over the meat. Cover and cook on low or high. Half-an-hour before serving, stir in the flour mixed with corn and correct seasoning with salt and pepper.

Low   8–10 hours
High   4–5 hours

Pork chops with rice

4–6 pork chops
2 tablespoons lard or vegetable shortening
1 onion, sliced
1 green pepper, seeded and cut into rings
salt and pepper
1 can (16oz.) tomatoes
1 cup pre-cooked, long grain rice

Brown the chops on both sides in the lard in a skillet. Drain on paper towels. Lightly fry the onion and pepper, place in the slow-cooking pot and arrange the chops on top. Sprinkle with salt and pepper. Add the tomatoes and cook on low. Turn to high, stir in the rice and cook for a further hour.

Low   6–8 hours

Pineapple glazed ribs

4–5lbs. spareribs, cut into two-rib pieces
salt and pepper
½ cup pineapple juice
2 tablespoons wine vinegar
¾ cup white wine
2 tablespoons soy sauce
2 tablespoons honey
1 tablespoon cornstarch
3 tablespoons cold water

Place spareribs on rack in shallow baking pan. Brown

in 400°F. oven for 30 minutes, turning ribs once. Remove from oven; pour off fat. Sprinkle ribs with salt and pepper. Place in slow-cooking pot. Combine remaining ingredients except cornstarch and water; pour over ribs. Cover and cook on low. Turn control to high. Dissolve cornstarch in cold water. Stir into rib mixture. Cook 10 to 15 minutes or until slightly thickened.

Low   7–9 hours

Veal chops Magyar

4–8 veal chops (depending on size)
salt and pepper
¼ cup all-purpose flour
2 tablespoons butter or margarine
1 onion, sliced
2 cups sliced large mushrooms
1 tablespoon sweet paprika
2oz. tomato paste
1¼ cups veal or chicken broth
juice of 1 lemon
⅔ cup light cream or half-and-half
paprika to garnish

Sprinkle chops with salt and pepper. Coat the chops with flour. Heat the fat in a skillet and brown the chops on both sides. Add the onions and fry until transparent. Put the mushrooms in the slow-cooking pot, add the onions, then the chops. Stir the paprika into the juices left in the skillet, stir in tomato paste, broth, salt, pepper and lemon juice and bring to a boil. Pour over chops. Cover and cook on low or high. Just before serving, pour over the cream and sprinkle with a little more paprika. Serve chops with sauce and boiled rice (cooked separately).

Low   6–8 hours
High   3–4 hours

Stuffed veal shoulder

2 cups soft white breadcrumbs
¼ cup shredded suet or chopped bacon
1 small green pepper, seeded and chopped
1 cup chopped mushrooms
1 tablespoon soy sauce
1 egg, beaten
salt and pepper
2–3lbs. shoulder of veal
2 tablespoons lard or vegetable shortening

Have veal shoulder boned. Mix breadcrumbs, suet, pepper, mushrooms, soy sauce, egg, salt and pepper. Spread mixture evenly over inside of boned veal. Roll

up and tie at intervals with string. Heat the lard in a skillet and brown the veal on all sides. Transfer to the slow-cooking pot and season with salt and pepper. Cover and cook on high.

The juices produced during cooking may be used as a gravy to serve with the veal. To thicken, stir in 2 teaspoons cornstarch mixed with 2 tablespoons water and cook on high for 30 minutes.

High   5–6 hours

Stuffed veal

4 slices of veal leg
I cup soft breadcrumbs
pinch of basil
pinch of sage
a little chopped parsley
$\frac{1}{2}$ onion, finely chopped
salt and pepper
$\frac{1}{4}$ cup corn oil
I can (10$\frac{3}{4}$oz.) condensed tomato soup
3 tablespoons white wine

Pound veal until thin. Mix the breadcrumbs, basil, sage, parsley, onion, salt and pepper. Moisten with enough corn oil to bind together. Spread an equal amount of stuffing over each piece of veal. Roll up and tie with string. Heat the remaining oil in a skillet, sauté the veal until golden brown then drain on paper towels. Transfer to the slow-cooking pot, add the soup, wine, salt and pepper. Cover and cook on low or high. Lift out the veal and remove the string. Serve veal with pan juices on a bed of rice, cooked separately.

Low   6–8 hours
High   3–4 hours

Veal with mushrooms

I$\frac{1}{2}$lbs. boneless stewing veal
2 tablespoons butter or margarine
I tablespoon oil
$\frac{1}{4}$lb. small white onions, peeled
$\frac{1}{2}$lb. button mushrooms, trimmed
I can (10$\frac{1}{2}$oz.) condensed cream of mushroom soup
salt and pepper
3 tablespoons light cream or milk

Cut the veal into I-inch cubes. Heat the butter and oil in a skillet, brown the veal and lightly brown the onions. Transfer to the slow-cooking pot and add the mushrooms and soup. Season with salt and pepper and

stir thoroughly. Cover and cook on low or high. Just before serving, stir in the cream or milk. Serve veal with sauce on boiled rice with a green vegetable.

Low   6–8 hours
High   3–4 hours

South Texas bean casserole

$\frac{3}{4}$lb. dried canellini beans
6 cups cold water
$\frac{1}{2}$lb. salt pork, rind removed and diced
Ilb. lean boneless chuck steak, cut into I-inch cubes
I red pepper
I medium-sized onion, chopped
2 cloves garlic, minced
I can (6oz.) tomato paste
I$\frac{1}{2}$ tablespoons chili powder
I teaspoon salt
I teaspoon cumin seed
$\frac{1}{2}$ teaspoon marjoram leaves

Soak beans in water overnight. Brown salt pork in skillet without any additional fat. Transfer to slow-cooking pot and mix soaked beans (with water), browned pork and remaining ingredients. Cover and cook on low.

Low   9–10 hours

Veal or pork birds

8 thin slices veal or pork leg
2 cups soft white breadcrumbs
$\frac{1}{2}$ cup grated Parmesan cheese
I tablespoon chopped Parsley
$\frac{1}{4}$ cup shredded suet or chopped bacon
salt and pepper
I egg, beaten
3 tablespoons milk
2 tablespoons butter or margarine
I$\frac{1}{4}$ cups chicken, pork or veal broth
chopped parsley to garnish

Sauce
2 tablespoons butter
$\frac{1}{4}$ cup all-purpose flour
I$\frac{1}{4}$ cups milk
$\frac{3}{4}$ cup grated Parmesan cheese
salt and pepper

Pound the slices of veal or pork until very thin. Mix the breadcrumbs, cheese, parsley, suet, salt and pepper. Stir in beaten egg and milk. Spread each slice

of veal or pork with a little stuffing, roll up and tie with string. Heat the butter in a skillet and brown the rolls lightly on all sides. Drain and transfer to the slow-cooking pot. Add the broth and a little salt and pepper. Cover and cook on low or high. When cooked, carefully drain off all liquid, adding $\frac{1}{2}$ cup to the milk for the sauce. Remove string and keep rolls hot on a heatproof pan while making the sauce.

Melt the butter in a saucepan, stir in the flour and cook for a few minutes. Remove from heat and gradually stir in the milk and broth. Bring to a boil for 2 minutes, stirring continuously. Stir in $\frac{1}{2}$ cup of the cheese and season to taste with salt and pepper. Pour sauce over the rolls and sprinkle remaining cheese on top. Brown under the broiler. Serve sprinkled with chopped parsley.

Low   6–8 hours
High   3–4 hours

NOTE: If you have a stoneware pot, leave rolls in pot and remove from base. Sprinkle with cheese and broil as above.

Veal suprême

1$\frac{1}{2}$lbs. boneless stewing veal
1 small onion, thinly sliced
3 ribs celery, chopped
2 carrots, sliced
bouquet garni (bay leaf, thyme, parsley)
salt and pepper
1$\frac{1}{4}$ cups veal, chicken or pork broth
1 tablespoon flour mixed with 2 tablespoons water
$\frac{1}{3}$ cup light cream

Cut the veal into 1-inch cubes. Place the onion, celery and carrots in the slow-cooking pot and place the veal on top. Add the bouquet garni, salt and pepper and broth. Cover and cook on low or high. To thicken the sauce, stir in the flour mixture half-an-hour before cooking time is complete. Just before serving, remove the bouquet garni and stir in the cream. Serve veal with sauce garnished with crisp bacon slices.

Low   8–10 hours
High   4–5 hours

Old-fashioned smoked pork dinner

2lbs. smoked pork shoulder or smoked tenderloin
few whole cloves
1 onion, finely chopped
1 apple unpeeled, cored and chopped

2lbs. even-sized new potatoes, washed but not peeled
1$\frac{1}{4}$ cups boiling light ale or water
salt and pepper

Remove wrapping or skin from pork. Stick cloves into the pork and place the pork in the slow-cooking pot with the onion and apple. Arrange the potatoes around the pork, then pour in the boiling liquid, salt and pepper. Cover and cook on high then low or high continuously. To serve, place the potatoes in a deep dish, remove the cloves from the pork, slice the pork thickly and lay on top of the potatoes. Boil the liquid rapidly in a separate pan until half its original volume. Pour over pork.

High   5–6 hours *or*
High   1 hour *then*
Low   8–10 hours

Boiled ham to serve cold

2lbs. smoked ham, shank end
1 tablespoon sugar
few whole peppercorns and whole cloves
bay leaf
5 cups boiling water
soft breadcrumbs sautéed in butter until crisp

Soak the ham for 30 minutes in cold water, drain and place in the slow-cooking pot with sugar, peppercorns, cloves, bay leaf and boiling water. Cover and cook on high then low or high continuously. When cooked, allow to cool in the liquid in the pot. When quite cold, remove the ham, draining it well. Remove the skin and serve sprinkled with browned breadcrumbs.

High   5–6 hours *or*
High   1 hour *then*
Low   8–10 hours

Liver and bacon

1lb. lambs' liver
$\frac{1}{4}$ cup all-purpose flour
salt and pepper
6 slices bacon
1 small onion, chopped
2 tablespoons lard or vegetable shortening
*$\frac{2}{3}$ cup beef broth
1 tablespoon flour mixed with 2 tablespoons water

Wash and dry the liver thoroughly. Cut into 1-inch thick slices and coat in flour mixed with salt and

pepper. Lightly fry the bacon and onion in the lard in a skillet. Drain well and place in the slow-cooking pot. Lightly fry liver and add to the pot with broth, salt and pepper. Cover and cook on low or high. To thicken the gravy stir in the flour mixture half-an-hour before cooking time is complete.

*Increase liquid to $1\frac{1}{4}$ cups when cooking on high.

Low   6–8 hours
High 3–4 hours

Country-style pâté

2 tablespoons butter
I small onion, chopped
$\frac{1}{2}$lb. lambs' liver, chopped
$\frac{1}{4}$lb. boneless lean pork
$\frac{1}{4}$lb. pork fat
I clove garlic, crushed
pinch of thyme
salt and pepper
little milk or brandy
$\frac{1}{4}$lb. bacon

In a skillet melt the butter and lightly fry the onion and liver. Grind with the pork, fat and garlic until

fine. Add thyme, salt, pepper and enough liquid to make a soft consistency. Stir in contents of skillet. Line a loaf pan or heatproof dish large enough to fit into slow-cooking pot, with bacon, fill with the pâté mixture and cover with foil. Stand in the slow-cooking pot and add enough hot water to come halfway up the container. Cover and cook on low. Leave to cool in the container, cover with a fresh piece of foil and a weight. Unmold and slice when cold and serve with hot toast.

Low   4–6 hours

Liver with sage sauce

$1\frac{1}{2}$lbs. lamb or pork liver
salt and pepper
2 tablespoons all-purpose flour
2 tablespoons butter or margarine
I medium-sized onion, finely chopped
I teaspoon sage
$1\frac{1}{4}$ cups hot beef broth
I tablespoon flour mixed with 2 tablespoons water

Cut the liver into thick slices, or get your butcher to do this for you. Wash and dry thoroughly. Sprinkle liver with salt and pepper. Coat in flour. Heat the

butter in a skillet and lightly brown the liver on both sides. Transfer to the slow-cooking pot with remaining ingredients except flour mixture. Cover and cook on low or high. To thicken the sauce, stir in the flour mixture half-an-hour before cooking time is complete.

Low   6–8 hours
High   3–4 hours

Roman liver

1½lbs. pork liver, sliced
¼ cup all-purpose flour
salt and pepper
2 tablespoons butter
1 tablespoon oil
1 medium-sized onion, chopped
½ teaspoon oregano
1 can (16oz.) tomatoes

Wash and dry the liver thoroughly. Coat in flour mixed with salt and pepper. Heat the butter and oil in a skillet, brown the liver and fry the onion until transparent. Drain and place into the slow-cooking pot, adding the oregano and tomatoes. Cover and cook on low or high. Serve with pasta, cooked separately.

Low   6–8 hours
High   3–4 hours

Coeur en casserole

1lb. beef heart
1 large onion, sliced
6 tablespoons butter
2 ribs celery, sliced
1 cup sliced mushrooms
3 tablespoons all-purpose flour
salt and pepper
1¼ cups hard cider
2 cooking apples
1 lemon
chives or watercress to garnish

Remove fat and gristle from the heart and slice thinly. Sauté onion in 2 tablespoons of the butter until soft. Place in the slow-cooking pot with the celery and mushrooms. Coat the heart in some of the flour mixed with salt and pepper and fry in the remaining butter until brown on all sides. Stir in the remaining flour. Stir in the cider. Place the heart mixture on top of the vegetables. Cover and cook on low or high. Peel and core the apples and slice thickly. Slice the lemon. One hour before the end of cooking time, place the apples, overlapping in a circle around the edge of the pot and press down lightly into the liquid. Place the lemon slices on top. Serve garnished with chopped chives or sprigs of watercress.

Low 10–12 hours
High 5–6 hours

Liver and bacon risotto

3 tablespoons oil
$\frac{3}{4}$lb. lamb liver, chopped
salt and pepper
1 tablespoon all-purpose flour
$\frac{1}{4}$lb. bacon, chopped
1 small onion, chopped
1 cup sliced button mushrooms
1 can (16oz.) tomatoes
$2\frac{1}{2}$ cups chicken, pork or veal broth
1 tablespoon Worcestershire sauce
$1\frac{1}{2}$ cups pre-cooked long grain rice

Heat the oil in a skillet. Sprinkle liver with salt and pepper. Toss the liver in the flour and lightly brown in the hot oil. Push liver to the side of the skillet and quickly fry the bacon, onion and mushrooms. Transfer the mixture to the slow-cooking pot and add the tomatoes, broth, Worcestershire sauce, rice, salt and pepper. Stir well. Cover and cook on low or high.

Low 6–8 hours
High 3–4 hours

Topped liver

$1\frac{1}{2}$lbs. pork liver
salt and pepper
$\frac{1}{4}$ cup all-purpose flour
$\frac{1}{4}$ cup butter
$1\frac{1}{2}$ cups sliced button mushrooms
1 cup white breadcrumbs
1 apple, peeled, cored and chopped
$\frac{1}{4}$ cup finely chopped shallots
1 teaspoon dried thyme
3 tablespoons butter, melted
*$\frac{2}{3}$ cup beef broth

Wash and dry the liver. Cut into thick slices and sprinkle with salt and pepper. Coat with flour. Heat the butter in a skillet and lightly brown the liver on both sides. Mix a third of the mushrooms with the breadcrumbs, chopped apple, shallots, thyme and melted butter. Divide stuffing equally between the liver slices, spreading almost to the edges. Roll up and fasten with a toothpick. Transfer to the slow-cooking

pot and add the remaining mushrooms, broth, salt and pepper. Cover and cook on low or high.

*Increase cooking liquid to $1\frac{1}{4}$ cups when cooking on high.

Low 6–8 hours
High 3–4 hours

Oxtail ragoût

2 oxtails, cut into 2-inch pieces
$\frac{1}{4}$ cup butter
1 tablespoon oil
1 onion, sliced
1 clove garlic, crushed
$\frac{1}{4}$lb. bacon, diced
4 carrots, sliced
4 ribs celery, chopped
salt and pepper
$1\frac{1}{4}$ cups beef broth
3 tablespoons red wine
$\frac{1}{2}$ teaspoon marjoram
chopped parsley to garnish

Wipe the oxtail pieces and brown in the butter and oil in a skillet. Drain on paper towels. Sauté the onion, garlic and bacon, drain. Place the carrots and celery in the slow-cooking pot, then the onions, oxtail and bacon. Season with salt and pepper. Add the broth, wine and marjoram. Cover and cook on low or high. Garnish with chopped parsley. Serve with boiled or creamed potatoes.

Low 10–12 hours
High 5–6 hours

William's ham

4 smoked ham slices, about $\frac{1}{2}$-inch thick
1 onion, chopped
2 carrots, grated
little black pepper
$1\frac{1}{4}$ cups hard cider

Trim fat from ham leaving $\frac{1}{4}$-inch edging; snip into this to prevent slices curling during cooking. Mix the onion, carrot and black pepper and place on the bottom of the slow-cooking pot. Arrange the slices on top, slightly overlapping and add the cider. Cover and cook on low or high. Serve with creamed parsley potatoes. (1 teaspoon chopped parsley and a large pinch of nutmeg into 2 cups creamed potatoes.)

Low 5–7 hours
High $2\frac{1}{2}$–$3\frac{1}{2}$ hours

Tripe with parsley sauce

1½lbs. tripe
1 large onion, cut into 8 pieces
1 large carrot, sliced
2 ribs celery, chopped
bay leaf
1¼ cups chicken broth
salt and pepper

Sauce
2 tablespoons margarine
¼ cup all-purpose flour
1¼ cups milk
salt and pepper
1 tablespoon chopped parsley

Wash tripe well. Cut into strips about 1-inch wide. Place in a large saucepan with the onion, carrot and celery. Cover with cold water and bring to a boil for 2 minutes. Skim well. Drain well and transfer to the slow-cooking pot. Add the bay leaf, broth, salt and pepper. Cover and cook on low or high. When cooked, drain off the cooking liquid, reserving ⅔ cup for the sauce.

Melt the margarine in a saucepan, stir in the flour and cook for 1–2 minutes. Remove from heat and gradually stir in the milk and cooking liquid. Return to heat and bring to a boil, stirring constantly. Season to taste with salt and pepper and stir in parsley. Pour sauce over tripe and vegetables.

Low   8–10 hours
High   4–5 hours

West country ham hocks

2lbs. ham hocks
1 medium-sized onion, sliced
2 leeks, sliced
2 carrots, sliced
bay leaf
2½ cups hot hard cider
2 teaspoons cornstarch mixed with 2 tablespoons
   water
chopped parsley to garnish

Soak the ham hocks for 1–2 hours in cold water, drain. Cover the ham hocks with water in a separate saucepan and bring to a boil. Drain carefully, removing all the scum. Place the hocks in the slow-cooking pot with the vegetables, bay leaf and hot cider. Cover and cook on high then low or high continuously. When cooked, remove the ham and keep hot. Skim excess fat from pan juices. Drain off half the liquid. Turn the slow-cooking pot to high and stir in the cornstarch mixture to thicken. Remove the skin from the hock and slice thickly. Return the sliced meat to the slow-cooking pot and sprinkle with a little chopped parsley.

High   5–6 hours *or*
High   1 hour *then*
Low   8–10 hours

Cold tongue

3lbs. smoked tongue
1 medium-sized onion, sliced
bouquet garni (bay leaf, scallions, parsley, thyme)
2 teaspoons vinegar or lemon juice
few peppercorns
1¼ cups boiling water

Place the washed tongue in the slow-cooking pot and add remaining ingredients. Cover and cook on high then low or high continuously. When cooked, remove the skin and any small bones and gristle. Roll the tongue and place into a bowl. Pour the cooking liquid into a saucepan and boil rapidly for 3–4 minutes to reduce it. Pour liquid over the tongue, cover with a plate and heavy weight and leave to set.

When cold, loosen edges and unmold. Garnish as desired.

High   6–7 hours *or*
High   1 hour *then*
Low   10–12 hours

Kidney stew

8–10 lambs' kidneys
1 small onion, chopped
2 tablespoons lard or vegetable shortening
½ cup sliced mushrooms
3 tablespoons tomato paste
⅔ cup beef broth
1 teaspoon chopped parsley
salt and pepper

Wash the kidneys, skin and cut in half, removing the tubes and fat. Lightly fry with the onion in the lard in a skillet. Transfer to the slow-cooking pot and add remaining ingredients. Cover and cook on low or high.

Low   6–8 hours
High   3–4 hours

Kidneys turbigo

8 pork kidneys
2 tablespoons butter or margarine
½ lb. pork sausages
¼ lb. small white onions
¼ lb. button mushrooms
3 tablespoons tomato paste
⅔ cup dry sherry
⅔ cup beef broth
salt and pepper
2 teaspoons cornstarch mixed with 1 tablespoon
   water
2 teaspoons chopped parsley to garnish

Skin and core the kidneys, cut in half lengthwise.
Heat the lard in a skillet and quickly brown the
kidneys, sausages and onions. Drain and transfer to
the slow-cooking pot; allow the sausages to cool
slightly and cut into bite-sized pieces before adding to
pot. Add the mushrooms, paste, sherry and broth,
stir well and season with salt and pepper. Cover and
cook on low or high. Half-an-hour before serving stir
in the cornstarch mixture and garnish with chopped
parsley.

Low   6–8 hours
High   3–4 hours

VEGETARIAN

Many of the recipes in this section are not for the true vegetarians as they include animal products such as cheese and eggs. However, they may tempt those of you who are not vegetarians to try a "meatless" dish occasionally—it can be just as tasty and nourishing. You may find too, that all the ingredients you require are already on your shelf.

Savory roast (see page 84) makes a tasty and economical meal and is just as good hot, or cold with a crisp salad. Navy or pea beans with cheese (see page 88) is a filling meal in itself and also makes an interesting vegetable accompaniment to pork or bacon.

Generally beans require soaking before being included in a recipe. This can either be done on the low setting overnight for about 8 hours, or if this is not convenient, cover with cold water, bring to a boil and boil for 2—3 minutes. Allow the beans to stand in the water for about 1 hour before draining and using. Dried beans are the main source of protein in vegetarian cooking. The amount of protein in nuts, dried beans and peas is very high—about the same as in meat, fish and cheese—and, although the proportion is diluted when the beans are soaked, they remain an excellent source of this nutrient.

Opposite: Vegetable canneloni (page 88)

Bean hotpot

½lb. dried navy or pea beans
1 medium-sized onion, thinly sliced
2 teaspoons dry mustard
salt and pepper
3 tablespoons molasses

Wash the beans, put into the slow-cooking pot, just cover with cold, salted water and leave on low overnight. Transfer the beans and liquid to a bowl. Put a layer of onion over the bottom of the slow-cooking pot and sprinkle with mustard. Add the beans and enough liquid to cover. Season with salt and pepper. Stir in molasses. Cover and cook on low.

Low   8–10 hours

Cheese and potato casserole

2lbs. potatoes
¼ cup butter
1 clove garlic, crushed
¼lb. American cheese slices
salt and pepper
1¼ cups cheese sauce

Slice the potatoes thinly and dry on paper towels. Grease the slow-cooking pot with 1 tablespoon of the butter. Melt the remaining butter. Cover the bottom of the pot with a layer of potatoes and a little of the melted butter. Add the garlic, half the cheese slices, salt and pepper. Repeat layers and pour sauce over top. Cover and cook on low.

Low   4–6 hours

Savory roast

1 can (16oz.) baked beans
2 cups soft white breadcrumbs
2 cups ½lb. grated Cheddar cheese
2 teaspoons fines herbes
1 small onion, finely chopped
1 tablespoon oil
1 egg, beaten
salt and pepper

Mash the beans in their sauce with the breadcrumbs. Stir in the cheese and herbs. Lightly sauté onion in the oil in a skillet then stir into the bean mixture with the egg, salt and pepper. Transfer to a lightly greased 2-cup casserole. Cover with foil and place in the

slow-cooking pot with about 1¼ cups cold water poured around it. Cover and cook on low or high. If serving cold, allow to cool in casserole, then unmold.

Low   6–8 hours
High   3–4 hours

Savory rice

1½ cups long grain rice
⅔ cup olive oil
1¼ cups tomato juice
1 cup finely sliced mushrooms
1¼ cups water
1 medium-sized onion, thinly sliced
1 green pepper, seeded and chopped
salt and pepper

In a skillet sauté the rice in the oil until golden brown. Place in the slow-cooking pot, draining off as much oil as possible. Add remaining ingredients, adding salt and pepper to taste, and stir well. Cover and cook on low. One hour before serving, stir again and season to taste with salt and pepper.

Low   5–6 hours

Eggs florentine

butter for greasing
2 packages (10oz. each) frozen leaf spinach, thawed, or 1½lbs. fresh cooked spinach

4 eggs
salt and pepper
$1\frac{1}{4}$ cups cheese sauce

Lightly grease the slow-cooking pot. Place an even layer of the well-drained spinach on bottom of pot. Using a cup or glass make 4 depressions in the spinach. Break an egg into each and season with salt and pepper. Pour cheese sauce evenly over the eggs. Cover and cook on low.

Low   3–4 hours

Macaroni and cheese

1 cup elbow macaroni
butter for greasing
large pinch of mustard
salt and pepper
$\frac{3}{4}$ cup (3oz.) grated Cheddar cheese
$1\frac{1}{4}$ cups cheese sauce

Cook macaroni in briskly boiling salted water until tender but still firm. Drain well. Place in a lightly greased slow-cooking pot. Mix the mustard, salt and pepper and half the cheese with the macaroni. Pour cheese sauce over macaroni and sprinkle with remaining cheese. Cover and cook on low.

Low   3–4 hours

Fruit and vegetable curry

1 tablespoon oil
4 ribs celery, chopped
1 onion, chopped
1 tablespoon curry powder
1 tablespoon all-purpose flour
$1\frac{1}{4}$ cups chicken broth or water
1 teaspoon ground ginger
juice and grated rind of 1 lemon
1 can (17oz.) apricot halves, drained
2 bananas, thickly sliced
1lb. cooking apples, peeled, cored and quartered
$\frac{1}{2}$ cup raisins
$\frac{2}{3}$ cup sour cream

Heat the oil in a skillet. Fry the celery and onion until lightly colored. Stir in the curry powder and flour and cook gently for a few minutes. Gradually stir in the liquid with the ginger. Place in the slow-cooking pot with the lemon juice and rind, apricots, bananas, apples and raisins. Stir thoroughly. Cover and cook on

Below : Fruit and vegetable curry

low or high. Just before serving, stir in the sour cream. Serve with plain rice and peanuts.

Low   4–6 hours
High   2–3 hours

Spinach castles

1lb. spinach
1 onion, diced
1 clove garlic, crushed
2 tablespoons butter
3 cups soft breadcrumbs
1 cup (4oz.) grated Cheddar cheese
1 teaspoon fines herbes
3 tablespoons chopped parsley
salt and pepper
1 egg
$\frac{1}{4}$–$\frac{1}{3}$ cup milk

Pre-heat the slow-cooking pot on high for 15 minutes. Wash the spinach and blanch in boiling salted water for 1 minute. Drain and cool. Sauté the onion and garlic in the butter in a skillet. Mix with the breadcrumbs, cheese, herbs and salt and pepper. Add the egg and enough milk to bind. Grease 6 custard cups and line them with spinach leaves. Press in the stuffing firmly and cover the top with remaining spinach. Cover each cup with greased foil. Place the cups in the slow-cooking pot and pour about $2\frac{1}{2}$ cups

85

boiling water around them. Cover and cook on low or high. When cooked, unmold on a warmed serving dish.

Low 4–6 hours
High 2–3 hours

Rice roulades

12 whole green cabbage leaves
$\frac{1}{2}$ cup long grain rice
$\frac{3}{4}$ cup chopped mushrooms
1 cup (4oz.) grated Cheddar cheese
1 teaspoon caraway seeds
1 tablespoon chopped parsley
salt and pepper
2 tablespoons butter

Wash the cabbage leaves carefully and cook in boiling salted water for 1 minute. Drain well. Cook the rice in boiling salted water for 20–25 minutes or until tender. Drain. Stir in mushrooms, half the cheese, caraway seeds and parsley, season well with salt and pepper. Divide equally between the leaves, spreading the filling over the surface of each leaf. Roll up lengthwise, turning in ends, and place side-by-side in the greased slow-cooking pot with 3 tablespoons water. Dot roulades with butter. Cover and cook on low or high. Sprinkle remaining cheese over the roulades.

Low 6–8 hours
High 3–4 hours

NOTE: If you have a stoneware pot, sprinkle food with cheese. Remove from base and brown under broiler.

Nut rice

1 onion, finely chopped
1 tablespoon oil
1 cup long grain rice
1 green pepper, seeded and thinly sliced
$\frac{3}{4}$ cup coarsely chopped walnuts
$\frac{3}{4}$ cup peanuts
$\frac{1}{4}$ cup raisins
$1\frac{1}{4}$ cups chicken broth
salt and pepper

In a small skillet fry the onion in the oil to soften. Mix all the ingredients in a slow-cooking pot with broth, salt and pepper. Cover and cook on low or high.

Low 6–8 hours
High 3–4 hours

Stuffed eggplants

2 large eggplants
$\frac{1}{3}$ cup oil
3 tablespoons butter
1 onion, sliced
4 tomatoes, skinned and sliced
1 clove garlic, crushed
3 tablespoons chopped parsley
salt and pepper
$\frac{2}{3}$ cup chicken broth
$2\frac{1}{2}$ cups soft white breadcrumbs
6 tablespoons (1$\frac{1}{2}$oz.) grated Cheddar cheese

Cut the eggplants in half lengthwise, slash the edges, sprinkle with salt and leave to stand upside down for 1 hour. Drain. Sauté the eggplants slowly in the oil in a skillet on cut side. Remove pulp, leaving a shell $\frac{1}{2}$-inch thick. Reserve shells. Chop the pulp. Heat butter and sauté the onion. Mix together pulp, onion, tomato, garlic and parsley. Season well with salt and pepper. Fill the reserved eggplant shells and place in the slow-cooking pot with the broth. Cover and cook on low. Place eggplant shells on a broiler pan, sprinkle with breadcrumbs and cheese. Broil until cheese is melted and lightly browned.

Low 4–6 hours

NOTE: If you have a stoneware pot, sprinkle food with crumbs and cheese, remove from base and brown under broiler.

Vegetarian bouillabaisse

1lb. potatoes, thinly sliced
1 onion, sliced
1 clove garlic, crushed
1 tablespoon oil
$\frac{1}{2}$lb. (about 2) tomatoes
$\frac{1}{2}$ teaspoon fennel seeds
pinch of thyme
salt and pepper
2 cups chicken broth
4 eggs
$\frac{1}{4}$ cup (1oz.) grated Cheddar cheese
chopped parsley to garnish

Place the potatoes in the bottom of the slow-cooking pot. Sauté the onion and garlic in the oil to soften, then add to the pot. Skin and quarter the tomatoes, remove the seeds and slice the flesh. Place in the pot with the fennel, thyme, salt and pepper. Pour broth over potatoes. Cover and cook on low. Break the 4 eggs into the bouillabaisse, sprinkle with cheese and

continue cooking on low. Serve garnished with parsley.

Low   6–8 hours plus $\frac{1}{2}$ hour for eggs

Vegetable canneloni

12 tubes canneloni
$\frac{1}{2}$lb. (about 2) tomatoes, skinned and chopped
1 cup (4oz.) grated Cheddar cheese
2 cups soft breadcrumbs
1 tablespoon chopped parsley
salt and pepper
1 egg, beaten
1 can (16oz.) tomatoes
1 teaspoon oregano

Blanch the canneloni in boiling salted water for 5 minutes until just soft. Drain, rinse in cold water, drain and dry. Mix fresh tomatoes, cheese, breadcrumbs, parsley, salt and pepper and egg. Fill the canneloni tubes and place in the greased slow-cooking pot. Chop the canned tomatoes in their juice, add the oregano and pour over the canneloni. Cover and cook on low.

Low   3–4 hours

Cheesy baked onions

6 medium-sized onions
1 cup 4oz. grated Cheddar cheese
1 cup soft white breadcrumbs
salt and pepper
$\frac{2}{3}$ cup hot beef broth

Peel the onions, place in boiling water for 2 minutes, drain well and cool slightly. Carefully remove the center of each onion (an apple corer is ideal for this). Mix the cheese, breadcrumbs and salt and pepper. Fill the center of each onion with the mixture, pressing it well down. Stand the onions in the slow-cooking pot and pour the hot broth over onions. Baste the onions as you do so. Cover and cook on low or high.

Low   6–8 hours
High   3–4 hours

Lentil stew

$\frac{1}{2}$lb. lentils
1 carrot, diced
2 leeks, thinly sliced
2 ribs celery, thinly sliced
1 onion, diced

1 can (16oz.) tomatoes
$\frac{1}{2}$ teaspoon fennel seeds
$\frac{2}{3}$ cup beef broth
salt and pepper
chopped parsley to garnish

Place the lentils in the slow-cooking pot with $2\frac{1}{2}$ cups water and cook on low overnight. Drain off any surplus liquid. Add the vegetables, tomatoes, fennel seeds, broth, salt and pepper. Cover and cook on low or high. Serve sprinkled with parsley.

Low   10–12 hours
High   5–6 hours

Navy or pea beans with cheese

1lb. dried navy or pea beans
2 onions, grated
2 large potatoes, grated
3 tablespoons chopped parsley
*$2\frac{1}{2}$ cups chicken broth
salt and pepper
1 cup (4oz.) grated Cheddar cheese

Wash the beans, put into the slow-cooking pot, just cover with cold salted water and leave on low overnight. Mix in the onion, potato, parsley, broth and salt and pepper. Cover and cook on low or high. Sprinkle top with grated cheese.

*Increase liquid to $3\frac{3}{4}$ cups if cooking on high.

Low   6–8 hours
High   3–4 hours

NOTE: If you have a stoneware pot, sprinkle food with cheese. Remove pot from base and broil until browned.

Cheese pudding

3 eggs, beaten
$1\frac{1}{2}$ cups soft breadcrumbs
$1\frac{1}{2}$ cups (6oz.) grated Cheddar cheese
salt and pepper
pinch of mustard
1 teaspoon fines herbes
1 onion, chopped
1 tablespoon oil
2 cups milk
2 tablespoons butter

Pre-heat the slow-cooking pot on high for 15 minutes.

Mix the eggs, breadcrumbs, I cup of the cheese, salt, pepper, mustard and herbs. Sauté the onion in the oil until soft and add to the mixture. Warm the milk and butter and pour over the mixture. Mix well. Pour into a greased 5-cup ovenproof dish. Cover with greased foil and stand in the slow-cooking pot. Add enough hot water to come halfway up the side of the dish. Cover and cook on high. Sprinkle with remaining cheese.

High   3–4 hours

NOTE: If you have a stoneware pot, sprinkle food with cheese. Remove pot from base and place under broiler to brown.

DESSERTS

How often do you hear the comments 'we all love desserts but don't have time to cook them' or 'it isn't worth putting the oven on just to cook a dessert'? We all know that time doesn't always allow us to economize by filling the oven. Let the slow-cooking pot come to the rescue. Baked desserts will cook quite happily for several hours; a delicious example is the Apple and chocolate pudding (see page 95).

Egg custard, crème caramel (page 92) and deliciously flavored custards are so good to eat but often tricky to make. The gentle, constant heat of a slow-cooking pot is ideal for these delicate desserts. Crème brulée is no longer a treat only to be enjoyed in expensive restaurants (see page 98).

When fruits such as rhubarb, apricots and plums are plentiful let the slow-cooking pot cook them gently, retaining their shape and flavor. Cooked like this, fruits are ideal for freezing, for use in flans and pies. Don't throw away the last of the bread, make Old-fashioned bread pudding (see page 93).

Opposite: Family fruit pie (page 100)

Baked apples

4 medium-sized cooking apples
$\frac{1}{3}$ cup mincemeat
2 tablespoons butter
$\frac{2}{3}$ cup water

Wash and dry apples. Make a shallow cut through the skin around the middle of each one. Remove the core. Stand the apples in the slow-cooking pot and fill the center of each with mincemeat. Top with a small pat of butter. Pour the water around them. Cover and cook on low or high.

Low   6–8 hours
High   3–4 hours

Crème caramel

6 tablespoons sugar
$\frac{1}{4}$ cup water
2 cups milk
2 large eggs, well beaten
few drops vanilla extract

Make the caramel by boiling together rapidly in a small open saucepan 4 tablespoons of the sugar and the water. When it is a deep golden color, divide equally between 4 warmed custard cups and quickly turn each cup so that the caramel coats the sides. Warm the milk, stir in the remaining sugar and beat into eggs. Stir in the vanilla. Strain into the lined cups. Pour $1\frac{1}{4}$ cups cold water into the slow-cooking pot. Place the cups into water. Cover and cook on low.

Low   6–8 hours

Castle puddings

$\frac{1}{2}$ cup butter or margarine
$\frac{1}{2}$ cup sugar
2 eggs, beaten
3 tablespoons milk
$1\frac{1}{2}$ cups self-rising flour
$\frac{1}{2}$ cup raspberry jam
$\frac{1}{3}$ cup flaked coconut to decorate

Pre-heat the slow-cooking pot on high for 15 minutes. Cream butter and sugar together until light and fluffy. Beat in the eggs, a little at a time. Beat in milk. Fold in the flour. Lightly grease 6 custard cups, divide jam equally between cups. Divide batter between the cups. Cover each with greased wax paper and then aluminum foil and tie with string Place the cups in the pot and pour approximately

$2\frac{1}{2}$ cups boiling water around them. Cover and cook on high. When cooked, turn out on a warmed serving dish and sprinkle with coconut.

High   2–3 hours

Cup custards

2 cups milk
3 tablespoons sugar
2 large eggs, well beaten
few drops vanilla extract
grated nutmeg

Warm the milk, stir in the sugar and beat into eggs. Stir in vanilla. Strain into 4 custard cups and sprinkle with nutmeg. Pour $1\frac{1}{4}$ cups cold water into the slow-cooking pot. Place the cups into the water. Cover and cook on low.

Low   6–8 hours

Rice pudding

6 tablespoons regular rice (do not use converted rice)
$\frac{1}{4}$ cup sugar
$3\frac{3}{4}$ cups milk
2 tablespoons butter
grated nutmeg
whipped cream to decorate (optional)

Lightly grease the slow-cooking pot. Wash the rice, put into pot with the sugar and milk and stir to mix ingredients thoroughly. Dot with small pieces of butter and sprinkle with nutmeg. Cover and cook on low. Stir to blend and serve warm or cold, topped with whipped cream.

Low   6–8 hours

Raisin pudding

1 cup self-rising flour
1 cup fine soft white breadcrumbs
$\frac{3}{4}$ cup shredded suet (about 3oz.)
$\frac{1}{4}$ cup sugar
$\frac{1}{2}$ cup raisins
$1\frac{1}{4}$ cups milk

Pre-heat the slow-cooking pot on high for 15 minutes. Mix the dry ingredients together, add enough milk to form a soft dough and place in a well-greased $2\frac{1}{2}$-cup bowl. Cover with greased wax paper and then aluminum foil. Tie securely in place with string. Place

the bowl in the slow-cooking pot and add boiling water to come half-way up the side of the bowl. Cover and cook on high. Serve with butter and brown sugar.

High 4–6 hours

Old-fashioned bread pudding

1 loaf (1lb.) firm-type white bread
2 cups milk
½ cup currants
¼ cup raisins
¼ cup chopped candied orange rind
¼ cup firmly packed light brown sugar
½ cup shredded suet, or ¼ cup vegetable shortening
2 teaspoons pumpkin pie spice
2 eggs, beaten
milk for mixing
brown sugar for topping

Slice the crusts from bread and cut remaining bread into cubes. Place in a large mixing bowl, cover with the milk and soak for ½–1 hour. Beat the bread pieces until almost smooth, then stir in remaining ingredients and enough milk to make the consistency of pancake batter. Pour into lightly greased slow-

cooking pot and sprinkle with a thin layer of brown sugar. Place aluminum foil or greased wax paper between the top of the pot and the lid. Cover and cook on low.

Low 3–4 hours

NOTE: If you have a stoneware pot, remove pot from base. Sprinkle the cooked pudding liberally with more brown sugar and melt this under the broiler until crisp.

Orange bread and butter pudding

8 slices bread
¼ cup butter
3 tablespoons orange marmalade
rind from 2 oranges, finely grated
pinch of cinnamon or nutmeg
2½ cups milk
3 tablespoons sugar
2 large eggs, beaten
brown sugar for topping

Cut the crusts off the bread and spread each slice with butter and marmalade. Put in two layers in lightly greased slow-cooking pot, with a sprinkling of orange rind and spices between each. Warm the milk in a separate pan, stir in the sugar and beat into eggs. Pour this mixture over the bread. Place a sheet of wax paper between the top of the slow-cooking pot and the lid. Cover and cook on low.

Low   3–4 hours

NOTE: If you have a stoneware pot, use this crisp topping. Remove stoneware pot from its base and remove lid. Sprinkle the cooked pudding with brown sugar and place under the broiler for a few minutes.

Pineapple upside-down cake

$\frac{1}{4}$ cup butter
I package (18$\frac{1}{2}$oz.) yellow cake mix
I can (14$\frac{1}{4}$oz.) pineapple slices
$\frac{1}{2}$ cup firmly packed brown sugar
12 maraschino cherries

Set the slow-cooking pot on high and heat the butter in pot until melted. Prepare cake mix according to the package directions, using the strained juice from the pineapple instead of water. When the butter is melted, use a little of it to grease the sides of the slow-cooking pot, then sprinkle the sugar evenly over

the bottom. Arrange the pineapple and cherries on top and spoon the cake mixture evenly over fruit. Cover and start cooking on high, then turn to low until firm and risen. Loosen edges. Invert the cake on warm serving dish.

High   I hour *then*
Low   3 hours

Stewed fruit

The slow-cooking pot is ideal for cooking fruit such as plums, apricots or rhubarb, particularly when retention of shape is important for making up fruit pies and flans.

The amount of sugar used should be adjusted according to the fruit and personal taste. Generally allow $\frac{2}{3}$ cup water to each 2 pounds of dried fruit. Cover and cook on low or high.

Low   5–6 hours
High   2$\frac{1}{2}$–3 hours

Rhubarb

2lbs. rhubarb
$\frac{1}{2}$ cup sugar
$\frac{2}{3}$ cup water

Wash rhubarb, cut into I-inch lengths. Place in slow-cooking pot with sugar and water. Cover and cook on low or high.

Low   5–6 hours
High   2$\frac{1}{2}$–3 hours

Apple snowballs

4 medium-sized cooking apples
3 tablespoons raspberry jam
2 crisp macaroons, crushed
$\frac{2}{3}$ cup water
2 tablespoons butter
2 egg whites
$\frac{1}{2}$ cup sugar
$\frac{1}{4}$ cup sliced almonds

Peel and core the apples. Mix the jam with the macaroons and fill the center of each apple with this mixture. Place the apples in the slow-cooking pot, add the water and dot the top of each apple with butter. Cover and start cooking on high. Baste the apples

well, then turn to low. Cover and cook on low.

Pre-heat the oven to 325°F. Transfer apples to shallow baking pan. Beat egg whites until stiff. Gradually beat in sugar, 1 tablespoon at a time, until stiff and glossy. Spread meringue over each apple covering completely. Sprinkle with almonds. Bake for 15–20 minutes or until lightly browned. Serve warm.

High ½ hour *then*
Low 3–4 hours

NOTE: If you have a stoneware pot, remove pot from base, remove lid and carefully drain off the liquid. Make meringue as above. Coat each apple with meringue and sprinkle with sliced almonds as above. Bake as above.

Apple and chocolate pudding

6 tablespoons butter
2½ cups finely crushed chocolate wafers or crackers
3 medium-sized cooking apples
butter or margarine for greasing
grated rind and juice of 1 lemon
3 tablespoons honey

Pre-heat the slow-cooking pot on high for 15 minutes. Melt the butter in a saucepan and stir in chocolate crumbs. Peel, core and slice the apples into ¼-inch thick slices. Lightly grease a 5-cup soufflé dish or other suitable container. Put half the apple slices in the bottom of dish, add half the lemon rind and juice and half the honey. Spread half the chocolate crumb mixture over the apples, pressing down lightly. Repeat layers. Cover dish with aluminum foil or lightly greased wax paper and stand in the pot. Add boiling water to come halfway up side of the dish. Cover and cook on low or high.

Delicious hot or cold; serve with whipped cream, ice cream or hot chocolate sauce.

Low 6–8 hours
High 3–4 hours

Pears in red wine

1¼ cups port or dry red wine
¼ cup sugar
6 medium-sized firm pears
rind of 1 lemon
little red food coloring

Put the wine and sugar in the slow-cooking pot. Heat

on high until the sugar is dissolved. Peel the pears, keeping whole and leaving stems on. Place in the pot turning to coat well. Add the lemon rind and food coloring. Cover and cook on low, turning occasionally to coat with the wine mixture.

Serve with the wine poured over the pears.

Low   4–6 hours

Summer pudding

1lb. soft berries such as strawberries or raspberries
   (about 1 quart)
$\frac{1}{4}$ cup butter
6–8 slices of toasting bread, crusts removed
butter for greasing
$\frac{1}{3}$ cup firmly packed brown sugar
whipped cream to decorate

Pre-heat the slow-cooking pot on high for 15 minutes. Prepare and wash fruit. Butter the bread slices on both sides. Lightly grease a 5-cup soufflé dish or bowl. Make alternate layers of bread and fruit in the dish, beginning and ending with a layer of bread. Sprinkle sugar over each layer of fruit and a little over the top layer of bread. Cover with aluminum foil or lightly greased wax paper. Stand the dish in the slow-cooking pot and add boiling water to come halfway up side of dish. Cover and cook on low or high. Serve hot with

hot fruit sauce or cream, or cool in dish covered with a weight.

Then turn out on a serving dish and decorate with whipped cream.

Low   4–6 hours
High   2–3 hours

Fruit compote

$\frac{1}{2}$lb. prunes
$\frac{1}{2}$lb. dried apricots
$\frac{1}{2}$lb. figs
$\frac{1}{2}$ cup raisins
1 cup dried apple rings
2 cups water
$\frac{2}{3}$ cup white wine
$\frac{1}{2}$ cup walnut pieces
$\frac{1}{2}$ cup whole blanched almonds

Place the fruits, water and wine in the slow-cooking pot. Cover and cook on low or high. Remove from pot, add nuts, cool and chill.

Serve with whipped or sour cream, or plain yogurt.

Low   5–6 hours
High $2\frac{1}{2}$–3 hours

Blueberry streusel cake

2 cups unsifted all-purpose flour
1 cup sugar
4 teaspoons baking powder
$\frac{1}{8}$ teaspoon salt
2 eggs, beaten
$\frac{1}{2}$ cup salad oil
$\frac{1}{4}$ cup milk
1 teaspoon vanilla extract
2 cups fresh or thawed frozen blueberries, drained
whipped cream and extra blueberries to decorate

In a mixing bowl combine flour, sugar, baking powder and salt. Add eggs, oil, milk and vanilla. Beat until smooth. Fold in blueberries. Pour into greased 2-quart mold. Cover mold with 4 or 5 paper towels. Place in slow-cooking pot. Cover and cook on high. Cool on rack for 5 minutes. Unmold onto plate.

Decorate with cream and blueberries.

High   3–4 hours

Chocolate dessert

butter or margarine for greasing
2 large eggs, or 2 medium eggs and 1 yolk
3 tablespoons cocoa
3 tablespoons sugar
few drops vanilla extract
2 cups milk
grated chocolate to decorate

Lightly grease a 3-cup soufflé dish or bowl. Beat the eggs with cocoa, sugar and vanilla extract. Heat milk to lukewarm, beat gradually into egg mixture. Strain into the dish and cover with aluminum foil or lightly greased wax paper. Stand the container in the slow-cooking pot and pour about $1\frac{1}{4}$ cups cold water around it. Cover and cook on low. Serve chilled decorated with grated chocolate and Orange cream.

Low   4–5 hours

Orange cream
1 cup ($\frac{1}{2}$ pint) whipping cream, whipped
grated rind of 1 orange
1 tablespoon whisky or brandy

Mix ingredients thoroughly and serve chilled.

Peach flambé

8 fresh peaches
⅓ cup firmly packed brown sugar
½ cup brandy

Skin the peaches by placing them in boiling water for 1 minute. Halve and remove pits. Place cut side down in the slow-cooking pot and cover with the brown sugar and 5 tablespoons of the brandy. Cover and cook on low or high. Spoon into serving dish. Just before serving, warm the remaining brandy. Set aflame and pour while flaming over peaches. Serve warm.

Low   3–4 hours
High   1½–2 hours

Lemon pudding

¼ cup butter or margarine
⅔ cup sugar
grated rind and juice of 2 lemons
3 tablespoons hot water
½ cup all-purpose flour
2 egg yolks
⅔ cup milk
2 egg whites, stiffly beaten

Pre-heat the slow-cooking pot on high for 15 minutes. Cream the butter, sugar and lemon rind until light and fluffy. Add the hot water and beat well. Stir in the flour. Beat the yolks into the mixture with the lemon juice and milk. Fold in the stiffly beaten egg whites. Pour into a greased 3-cup ovenproof dish. Cover with a double thickness of greased wax paper or aluminum foil. Place the dish in the slow-cooking pot and pour 1¼ cups hot water around it. Cover and cook on high. Serve hot with whipped cream or chill and decorate with grated chocolate.

High   3–4 hours

Apple brown betty

¼ cup butter or margarine
4 cups soft breadcrumbs
1 teaspoon cinnamon
juice and grated rind of 1 orange
⅔ cup brown sugar
4 cooking apples, peeled, cored and sliced

Melt the butter, stir in the breadcrumbs, cinnamon and orange rind. Lightly grease the slow-cooking pot and sprinkle 2 tablespoons of the sugar on the bottom. Arrange half the sliced apples in the pot, pour over half the orange juice and sprinkle with ¼ cup of the sugar and half the buttered crumbs. Repeat the layers and press down firmly. Cover and cook on low. Sprinkle remaining sugar on top of the pudding and serve warm.

Low   4–5 hours

NOTE: If you have a stoneware pot, remove pot from base. Sprinkle sugar on top as above and place under broiler to brown and crisp the top.

Spiced chocolate chip puddings

½ cup butter
½ cup sugar
2 eggs, beaten
3 tablespoons milk
1¼ cups self-rising flour
¼ cup cocoa
½ teaspoon pumpkin pie spice
½ cup chocolate chips

Pre-heat the slow-cooking pot on high for 15 minutes. Cream the butter and sugar together until light and fluffy. Beat in the eggs a little at a time. Beat in milk. Fold in the flour, cocoa, spice and chocolate chips. Lightly grease 6 custard cups and divide the mixture between them. Cover each with greased wax paper or aluminum foil and tie with string. Place in the slow-cooking pot and pour about 2½ cups boiling water around them. Cover and cook on high. When cooked, turn out on a warmed serving dish and pour Quick chocolate sauce over pudding.

High   2–3 hours

Quick chocolate sauce
Beat 1 package instant chocolate pudding with 3 cups cold milk. Set aside until slightly thickened. Stir in 1 teaspoon vanilla extract. Chill.

Crème brûlée

2½ cups heavy cream
vanilla extract
4 egg yolks
⅓ cup superfine sugar

Heat the cream and vanilla to scalding point in a saucepan. Beat egg yolks with 1 tablespoon of the sugar until light in color and creamy. Beat cream slowly into yolks. Return mixture to the pan and cook

over a very low heat, stirring constantly. Do not boil. Cook only until it coats the back of a wooden spoon. Strain the mixture into a shallow ovenproof dish and place in the slow-cooking pot. Pour enough cold water into the pot to come halfway up the sides of the dish, cover and cook on low. Remove from slow-cooking pot and allow the cream to chill for several hours or overnight. Sprinkle the top of the cream evenly with remaining sugar and place under hot broiler 4 inches away from heat. The sugar should melt before it caramelizes to form an even crusty coating over the surface. Chill again. Serve with berries such as raspberries or strawberries.

Low   2–3 hours

Date pudding

1 package (8oz.) pitted dates
$\frac{1}{4}$ cup sugar
$\frac{1}{2}$ cup chopped suet
$\frac{1}{2}$ cup self-rising flour
1 cup soft breadcrumbs
$\frac{1}{2}$ teaspoon pumpkin pie spice
1 egg
milk to mix

Pre-heat the slow-cooking pot on high for 15 minutes. Chop the dates. Mix sugar, suet, flour, breadcrumbs and spice. Add the dates, egg and enough milk to make the consistency of muffin batter. Pour into a well greased 3-cup bowl. Cover with greased wax

paper or aluminum foil. Place the bowl in the slow-cooking pot and add boiling water to come halfway up the side of the bowl. Cover and cook on high. Serve with custard sauce.

High   3–4 hours

Chocolate pear upside-down cake

$\frac{1}{4}$ cup butter, melted
$\frac{1}{3}$ cup brown sugar
2 teaspoons cinnamon
2 pears
8 candied cherries
$\frac{1}{2}$ cup butter or margarine
$\frac{1}{2}$ cup sugar
2 eggs, well beaten
$\frac{3}{4}$ cup self-rising flour
$\frac{1}{4}$ cup cocoa

Pre-heat the slow-cooking pot on high for 15 minutes. Use a little of the melted butter to grease a 5-cup soufflé dish or casserole. Stir the brown sugar and cinnamon into the remaining butter. Spread mixture evenly on the bottom of the dish. Peel and halve the pears, remove core. Place a cherry in each pear half and place these cut side down in dish. Put the remaining cherries between the pears. Cream the butter and sugar until light and fluffy. Beat in the eggs a little at a time. Fold in the flour and cocoa. Spread over the top of the pears as evenly as possible. Cover with wax paper and tie down. Place the dish in the slow-cooking pot and pour enough boiling water to come halfway up the sides of the dish. Cover and cook on high. When cooked, invert the cake on a warm serving dish.

High   2–3 hours

Family fruit pie

Any fruits may be used for the filling except apples on their own, which tend to discolor during the long slow cooking; however, they make an interesting combination with other fruits such as rhubarb or the old favorite, blackberries.

1lb. cooking apples
1 teaspoon lemon juice
½ teaspoon ground cinnamon
¼ cup firmly packed brown sugar
1lb. rhubarb
⅔ cup water
½ package (11oz.) pie crust mix, prepared according
   to package directions

Peel, core and slice the apples thickly. Make a layer on the bottom of the slow-cooking pot, add lemon juice, cinnamon and half the sugar. Wash the rhubarb, and cut into 1-inch lengths. Add to the pot with remaining sugar and water. Cover and cook on low or high. Pour mixture into a shallow casserole. Roll out the pie crust to fit the casserole. Moisten the side edge of the casserole with water, lay the pie crust over the fruit, press lightly against the sides and make a steam hole in the center. Bake in a hot oven (400°F.) for 30–40 minutes, until the pie crust is crisp and golden brown.

Low   3–5 hours
High   1½–2½ hours

NOTE: If you have a stoneware pot, leave apples in pot. Remove pot from base. Cover with pie crust and bake as above.

English Christmas pudding

The slow-cooking pot makes delicious Christmas puddings. The long cooking time allows them to be cooked overnight if you wish; an extra hour or so will not harm them, but will darken them a little more. Two-and-one-half cups water is enough to last many hours longer than the cooking time given below, so

there is no need to worry about replacing it during cooking.

This mixture will make 6 or 7 individual puddings in custard cups or two 2½-cup bowls (these have to be cooked one at a time).

Metal pudding pans should be lined with wax paper to prevent the acid in the fruit pitting the metal during storage.

½ cup all-purpose flour
pinch salt
2 teaspoons pumpkin pie spice
½ cup currants
1 cup raisins
½ cup chopped mixed candied fruits
1 cup shredded suet
½ cup firmly packed brown sugar
2 cups soft fine white breadcrumbs
½ cup chopped blanched almonds
grated rind of 1 lemon
2 eggs, beaten
3 tablespoons molasses
1 tablespoon brandy
a little stout, ale or milk for mixing

Sift the flour, salt and spice. Stir in fruits, suet, brown sugar, crumbs, almonds and lemon rind. Stir the eggs, molasses and brandy with enough stout to make the consistency of fruitcake dough. Divide between the greased containers, leaving about ½-inch head-space. Cover with a double thickness of greased wax paper or aluminum foil. Pre-heat the slow-cooking pot on high for 15 minutes. Stand the containers in pot and pour 2½ cups boiling water around them. Cover and cook on high then low, or high continuously.

Individual Puddings:
High   1 hour *then*
Low   10 hours *or*
High   6 hours

2½-cup Puddings:
High   1 hour *then*
Low   12 hours *or*
High   7 hours

Cool the puddings and cover with fresh wax paper or foil for storage.

TO RE-HEAT: Pre-heat the slow-cooking pot on high for 15 minutes. Stand the containers in the slow-cooking pot and pour hot water around them. Cover and heat on high. (The low setting may also be used, but double the cooking times listed below.)

Individual Puddings:
High   1½–2 hours

2½-cup Puddings:
High   3 hours

AROUND THE WORLD

Slow cooking is used all over the world. In China, for example, red-cooking and clear simmering are two traditional ways of cooking meat and vegetables for many hours, often in large earthenware pots and in delicious piquant sauces. Red-cooked lamb (see page 108) is taken from a traditional Chinese recipe and is ideally suited to the slow-cooking pot.

Many famous international dishes such as Osso bucco (see page 108) or Cassoulet (see page 112) are traditionally cooked very slowly and their individuality is often achieved by the use of herbs and spices from the country or regions of origin.

Holidays abroad give us the opportunity of trying many international dishes, cooked in the local way. When home again, we can recreate these dishes and enjoy a really cosmopolitan selection.

Opposite: Red-cooked lamb (page 108)

Malayan beef and shrimp soup (Malaya)

2 medium-sized onions
1 clove garlic, crushed
1lb. beef, cut into ½-inch cubes
2 tablespoons butter
1 teaspoon ground ginger
1 teaspoon turmeric
1 teaspoon ground coriander
5 cups hot water or chicken broth
1 package (8oz.) frozen shelled and deveined shrimp, thawed
1 tablespoon lemon juice
salt

Chop one onion finely and fry with the garlic and meat in the butter in a skillet. Place in the slow-cooking pot with the spices and water or broth. Cover and cook on low or high. Half-an-hour before serving, stir in the shrimp and lemon juice, add salt to taste. Slice the remaining onion into rings, fry until crisp in oil. Serve soup topped with crisp onions.

Low   6–8 hours or overnight
High   3–4 hours

Below: Boeuf catalan

sauce through a strainer or whirl in a blender. Reheat sauce in a saucepan and season to taste with salt and pepper. Pour sauce over the beef.

High   ½ hour, *then*
Low   6–8 hours

Boeuf catalan (France)

2lbs. top round (boneless)
oil or lard for frying
4 slices Canadian bacon, chopped
1 medium-sized onion, sliced
2 carrots, sliced
½ cup sliced mushrooms
1 clove garlic, crushed
bouquet garni (parsley, scallions, thyme, tarragon)
pinch of nutmeg
1 cup canned tomatoes
1 teaspoon molasses
1¼ cups hard cider
salt and pepper

Brown the beef on all sides in a skillet, drain on paper towels. Lightly fry the bacon, onion and carrots, drain excess fat, place in slow-cooking pot. Add the mushrooms, garlic, bouquet garni and nutmeg. Place the beef on top. Mix the tomatoes, molasses, cider, salt and pepper and pour over the beef. Cover and cook on high then low. Lift the beef onto a warmed serving dish; leave whole or cut into thick slices. Remove the bouquet garni and push the

Hungarian goulash (Hungary)

1½lbs. beef chuck, cut into 1-inch cubes
salt and pepper
¼ cup all-purpose flour
2 tablespoons lard or drippings
1 medium-sized onion, chopped
1 green pepper, seeded and chopped
1 tablespoon sweet paprika
3 tablespoons tomato paste
large pinch nutmeg
1¼ cups beef broth
⅔ cup plain yogurt

Sprinkle beef with salt and pepper. Roll cubes in flour. Heat the lard in a skillet and fry the beef until lightly browned. Place in slow-cooking pot. Sauté the onion and pepper until soft and add to the beef. Stir in paprika, tomato paste, nutmeg and broth. Cover and cook on low or high. Just before serving, stir in the yogurt and season to taste with salt and pepper.

Low   8–10 hours
High   4–5 hours

Boeuf flamande (France)

2lbs. boneless sirloin steak, in a piece
salt and pepper
2 tablespoons butter
4–6 slices bacon, chopped
2 medium-sized onions, sliced
$\frac{1}{4}$ cup cider vinegar
1 tablespoon molasses
bay leaf
2 whole cloves
$\frac{2}{3}$ cup ale or stout
1 tablespoon flour mixed with 2 tablespoons water

Pound steak and flatten to $\frac{1}{2}$-inch thickness. Season with salt and pepper, roll up like a jelly roll and tie with string. Heat the butter in a skillet and brown the roll on all sides. Drain on paper towels. Lightly fry the bacon and onion and place in the slow-cooking pot. Stir in the vinegar, molasses, bay leaf, cloves, ale, salt and pepper. Cover and cook on high then low or continuously on high. Half-an-hour before serving stir in the flour mixture and season to taste with salt and pepper. To serve, slice the meat on a warm dish and pour sauce over slices. Remove bay leaf before serving.

High $\frac{1}{2}$ hour, *then*
Low   6–8 hours *or*
High 3–4 hours

Mexican chicken (Mexico)

4 chicken quarters
salt and pepper
$\frac{1}{4}$ cup lard or vegetable shortening
1 large onion, chopped
1 clove garlic, crushed
1 red pepper, seeded and sliced
$\frac{1}{4}$ cup all-purpose flour
$\frac{2}{3}$ cup water
1 tablespoon tomato paste
1 tablespoon vinegar
1 teaspoon sugar
3 tablespoons dry sherry
$\frac{1}{2}$ teaspoon chili powder
few whole cloves
3 tablespoons seedless raisins
few green pitted olives, halved

Skin the chicken if preferred, dust well with salt and pepper. Heat the lard in a skillet and fry the onion and garlic gently until transparent. Drain and place in the slow-cooking pot. Brown the chicken in skillet and add to the pot with the red pepper. Drain off all but 1 tablespoon of the drippings in pan. Stir in the flour and cook for a few minutes. Mix the water, paste, vinegar, sugar, sherry, chili powder and cloves. Stir into the skillet. Cook until thickened then add the raisins and olives. Pour sauce over the chicken. Cover and cook on low or high. Serve with boiled rice.

Low   8–10 hours
High 4–5 hours

Stiffado (Greece)

1$\frac{1}{2}$lbs. beef chuck
2 tablespoons lard or vegetable shortening
2 cloves garlic, crushed
1$\frac{1}{4}$ cups tomato juice
3 tablespoons red wine
large pinch of coriander
salt and pepper

Cut the beef into 1-inch cubes. Heat the lard in a skillet and brown the beef. Add the garlic for the last few minutes of frying. Place in slow-cooking pot and stir in tomato juice, wine, coriander, salt and pepper. Cover and cook on low or high. Serve spooned over rice.

Low   10–12 hours
High 5–6 hours

Chinese pears (France)

6 firm pears
$\frac{1}{2}$ cup raisins
$\frac{3}{4}$ cup chopped walnuts
$\frac{1}{2}$ teaspoon cinnamon
$\frac{1}{2}$ teaspoon ground ginger
1 tablespoon honey
$\frac{1}{2}$ teaspoon cinnamon
1$\frac{1}{4}$ cups red wine

Peel the pears and cut a small slice from the bottom of each to enable it to stand upright. Slice a 1-inch piece from the top of each pear. Scoop out the core and seeds. Mix the raisins, nuts, spices and honey together and spoon into the pear cavities. Replace the lids. Stand the pears in the slow-cooking pot. Mix the cinnamon with the red wine and pour over the pears. Cover and cook on low or high. Serve hot or cold with whipped cream.

Low   4–6 hours
High 2–3 hours

Beef stroganoff (Russia)

1½lbs. sirloin steak
2 tablespoons butter
I small onion, finely chopped
⅔ cup beef broth
salt and pepper
2 cups thinly sliced mushrooms
⅔ cup sour cream, or ⅔ cup light cream mixed with
    I tablespoon lemon juice
chopped parsley to garnish

Trim the steak and wipe with a damp cloth. Cut steak into ½-inch wide slices. Heat the butter in a skillet and fry the steak and onion until lightly browned. Pour contents of skillet into slow-cooking pot and add the broth, salt and pepper. Cover and cook on low or high. Half-an-hour before serving, stir in the mushrooms. Just before serving, stir in the cream and season to taste with salt and pepper. Garnish thickly with parsley.

Low   6–7 hours
High   3–3½ hours

Figs in honey and wine (Greece)

Ilb. dried figs
1¼ cups sweet white wine
⅔ cup honey

Place all the ingredients in the slow-cooking pot. Cover and cook on low. Chill well. Serve with cream.

Low   7–9 hours

Caribbean bananas (Caribbean)

2 tablespoons butter
6–8 firm bananas (use bananas with yellow skin and
    green tips)
¼ cup firmly packed brown sugar
⅓ cup flaked coconut
6 tablespoons rum
⅓ cup water

Grease the slow-cooking pot well with the butter. Peel the bananas and slice in half lengthwise. Mix the

sugar and coconut. Place the bananas in the slow-cooking pot, layering them with the sugar and coconut mixture, reserving enough to sprinkle over the top. Pour the rum and water over bananas and sprinkle with remaining sugar and coconut. Cover and cook on low or high. Serve hot with whipped cream.

Low   4–6 hours
High   2–3 hours

Chili-con-carne (Mexico)

2 tablespoons butter or margarine
Ilb. ground chuck
I medium-sized onion, chopped
I small green pepper, seeded and chopped
2 ribs celery, chopped
2 teaspoons chili powder
salt and pepper
I can (16oz.) tomatoes
I can (15¼oz.) red kidney beans, drained

Heat the butter in a skillet and brown the beef. Drain excess fat. Place in slow-cooking pot. Add remaining ingredients and stir well. Cover and cook on low or high. Season to taste with salt and pepper.

Low   6–8 hours
High   3–4 hours

Barbecued spareribs (China)

2 tablespoons oil
12 pork spareribs (about 2–3lbs.)
I clove garlic, crushed
I medium-sized onion, finely chopped
¼ cup soy sauce
¼ cup dry sherry
I teaspoon Tabasco sauce
½ teaspoon paprika
½ teaspoon dry mustard
⅓ cup wine vinegar
salt and pepper

Heat the oil in a skillet and brown the spareribs, garlic and onion. Drain excess fat and place in the slow-cooking pot. Mix remaining ingredients, adding salt and pepper to taste, and pour over the pork. Cover and cook on low or high.

Low   6–8 hours
High   3–4 hours

Oeufs en cocotte à la crème (France)

⅓ cup light cream
⅓ cup grated Cheddar cheese
⅓ cup white wine
2 teaspoons lemon juice
2 teaspoons prepared mustard
salt and pepper
4 eggs

Mix the cream, cheese, wine, lemon juice and mustard, add a little salt and pepper. Lightly grease 4 custard cups and break 1 egg into each. Cover the eggs with the cream mixture. Place the cups in the slow-cooking pot and pour 1¼ cups water around them. Cover and cook on low or high.

Low   2 hours
High   1 hour

Variations

Tomato
½lb. (about 2) tomatoes, skinned and quartered
3 tablespoons tomato paste
4 eggs
salt and pepper
½ cup light cream
3 tablespoons chopped parsley

Remove seeds and slice tomatoes thinly. Place in 4 greased custard cups. Spoon in tomato paste. Break 1 egg into each cup. Season with salt and pepper. Mix the cream and parsley and spoon over the eggs. Cover and cook as above.

Fish
½lb. smoked haddock, flaked
4 eggs
salt and pepper
½ cup heavy cream

Place half of fish in the bottom of 4 greased custard cups, followed by 1 egg and salt and pepper. Top with remaining fish. Top with cream, cover and cook as above

Asparagus
1½ cups drained cooked asparagus pieces
4 eggs
salt and pepper
½ cup heavy cream

Place half of chopped asparagus in the bottom of 4 greased custard cups, followed by 1 egg and salt and pepper. Top with remaining asparagus. Top with the cream, cover and cook as above.

Red-cooked lamb (China)

'Red cooking' is a traditional Chinese method of slow cooking. Soy sauce is the predominant flavoring ingredient, followed by dry sherry, ginger, garlic and onion. Pork, beef and poultry can all be used for this recipe.

3lbs. shoulder of lamb, boned and cubed
salt and pepper
3 tablespoons oil
1 onion, chopped
1 clove garlic, crushed
¼ cup soy sauce
⅓ cup dry sherry
2 teaspoons sugar
⅔ cup beef broth
2 slices root ginger
2 bay leaves
2 teaspoons cornstarch mixed with 1 tablespoon water
1 small red pepper, thinly sliced

Season the lamb with salt and pepper. Heat the oil in a skillet, brown the lamb and sauté the onion and garlic until transparent. Drain excess fat and place in slow-cooking pot. Mix the soy sauce, sherry, sugar and broth. Pour over the lamb and mix well. Add the root ginger and bay leaves. Cover and cook on low or high. Half-an-hour before serving, stir in the cornstarch mixture. Just before serving, remove root ginger and bay leaves, and sprinkle with sliced pepper. Serve with prawn crackers or rice.

Low   8–10 hours
High   4–5 hours

Osso bucco (Italy)

6 pieces shin of veal, about 2-inches thick
salt and pepper
2 tablespoons butter or margarine
1 tablespoon oil
1 onion, sliced
1 clove garlic, crushed
2 carrots, sliced
½lb. tomatoes, skinned and chopped, *or* 1 cup canned tomatoes
3 tablespoons tomato paste
⅔ cup dry white wine
1 tablespoon chopped parsley to garnish

Season the veal with salt and pepper. Heat the butter and oil in a skillet and brown the veal. Drain and place in slow-cooking pot. Lightly sauté the onion, garlic

and carrots and add to the veal with the tomatoes, tomato paste and wine. Cover and cook on low or high. Sprinkle with chopped parsley and serve with saffron rice.

Low 6–8 hours
High 3–4 hours

Chicken vindaloo (India)

4 chicken quarters
salt and pepper
¼ cup lard or vegetable shortening
1 onion, sliced
3 tablespoons curry powder
1 teaspoon chili powder
1 tablespoon all-purpose flour
3 tablespoons wine vinegar
1¼ cups chicken broth
sprig fresh thyme
2 bay leaves

Skin the chicken quarters and season with salt and pepper. Heat the lard in a skillet, brown the chicken and fry the onion until transparent. Drain and place in slow-cooking pot. Stir the curry powder, chili powder and flour into the skillet juices. Remove from heat, stir in the vinegar and broth, return to heat and

bring to a boil. Pour sauce over the chicken. Add the thyme and bay leaves. Cover and cook on low or high. Remove bay leaves.

Low 7–9 hours
High 3½–4½ hours

Sweet and sour pork (China)

1½lbs. boneless pork, cut into ¾-inch cubes
salt and pepper
3 tablespoons cornstarch
3 tablespoons oil
1 onion, chopped
1 green pepper, seeded and thinly sliced
3 tablespoons soy sauce
3 tablespoons firmly packed brown sugar
3 tablespoons cider vinegar
3 tablespoons dry sherry
3 tablespoons tomato paste
3 tablespoons orange juice
¼ cup water

Season pork with salt and pepper. Roll pork in cornstarch, reserving any excess. Heat the oil in a skillet, brown the pork and lightly sauté the onion and green pepper. Stir in the soy sauce and place in the slow-cooking pot. Stir the remaining cornstarch into the skillet juices. Mix remaining ingredients, stir into skillet and bring to a boil. Pour sauce over the pork and vegetables. Cover and cook on low or high.

Low   8–10 hours
High 4–5 hours

Cantonese dinner (Far East)

2lbs. pork tenderloin
2 tablespoons lard or vegetable shortening
I medium-sized onion, chopped
I small green pepper, seeded and sliced
I cup sliced mushrooms
2 ribs celery, chopped
3 tablespoons firmly packed brown sugar
2 teaspoons Worcestershire sauce
I can (10¾oz.) condensed cream of celery soup
salt and pepper

Cut the pork into strips about I-inch wide. Heat the lard in a skillet and quickly brown the pork. Place pork in slow-cooking pot. Lightly sauté the onion, pepper, mushrooms and celery in skillet drippings. Pour into pot with meat and add remaining ingredients. Stir well. Cover and cook on low or high. Just before serving stir well and season to taste with salt and pepper.

Low   8–10 hours
High 4–5 hours

Paella (Spain)

I cup diced cooked chicken
½ cup cooked mussels, removed from shell
I small onion, finely chopped
I clove garlic, crushed
I green pepper, seeded and chopped
4 tomatoes, skinned and chopped
2 cups pre-cooked long grain rice
3 cups chicken broth
salt and pepper
large pinch powdered saffron
I cup frozen peas, thawed, or canned peas
I cup cooked, shelled and deveined shrimp

Place all ingredients except peas and shrimp in the slow-cooking pot and stir well. Cover and cook on low or high. Half-an-hour before serving, stir in the peas and shrimp.

Low   6–8 hours
High 3–4 hours

Sesame chicken with spiced rice (Japan)

½ cup all-purpose flour
1 tablespoon sesame seeds
½ teaspoon ginger
salt and pepper
4 chicken quarters
¼ cup butter
1 tablespoon oil
1¼ cups chicken broth
⅓ cup white wine
¾ cup long grain rice
½ teaspoon ground coriander
¼ teaspoon ginger
pinch chili powder
2 tablespoons butter

Mix the flour, sesame seeds, ginger, salt and pepper. Coat the chicken quarters with the mixture and reserve remaining flour mixture. Fry until golden in the butter and oil in a skillet. Drain and place in the slow-cooking pot. Stir the remaining flour mixture into drippings in skillet. Add the broth and wine and stir until thickened. Pour sauce over the chicken, cover and cook on low or high. Put the rice in a saucepan with 2½ cups cold water and 1 teaspoon salt. Bring to a boil, stir, then simmer for 15–20 minutes until tender. Drain and rinse with boiling water. Mix rice with spices and butter. Pile rice on to a warmed serving dish, arrange cooked chicken and sauce on top.

Low   8–10 hours
High   4–5 hours

Cassoulet (France)

1lb. dried navy or pea beans
bay leaf, crushed
2 cloves garlic, crushed
½ teaspoon thyme
½ teaspoon sage
salt and pepper
1lb. boneless pork, cubed
1lb. pork sausages
2 cups soft breadcrumbs
½ cup (2oz.) grated Cheddar cheese

Place the beans in the slow-cooking pot with enough water to cover and cook overnight on low until softened. Drain well. Stir in the bay leaf, garlic, thyme, sage, salt, pepper, pork and 2½ cups water. Brown the sausages in a skillet and place in a star shape on the top of the beans. Cover and cook on low. Pour beans and meat into a casserole. Sprinkle

the cheese and breadcrumbs over the top and brown under the broiler. Serve with sliced roast duck or chicken.

Low   8–10 hours

NOTE: If you have a stoneware pot, remove pot from base. Sprinkle beans with breadcrumbs and cheese. Broil as above.

Coq au vin (France)

1 chicken, 2–3lbs., cut-up
2 tablespoons butter
¼lb. shallots
¼lb. bacon, chopped
¼lb. small button mushrooms
salt and pepper
1¼ cups red wine
bouquet garni (thyme, rosemary, parsley, chives)

Wash chicken and pat dry. Remove skin. Heat the butter in a skillet and fry the chicken until light golden brown. Drain and place in the slow-cooking pot. Lightly fry shallots, bacon and mushrooms. Add to the pot with the salt, pepper, wine and bouquet garni. Cover and cook on low or high. Remove bouquet garni before serving.

Low   8–10 hours
High   4–5 hours

Veal in marsala (Italy)

2lbs. boneless stewing veal, cut into 1-inch cubes
salt and pepper
2 tablespoons lard or vegetable shortening
1 clove garlic, crushed
1 red pepper, seeded and sliced
large pinch of sage
⅔ cup Marsala
⅔ cup chicken broth or water
1 tablespoon cornstarch mixed with 2 tablespoons
   water for thickening
1 teaspoon chopped parsley to garnish

Season the veal with salt and pepper. Heat the lard in a skillet, brown the veal quickly and evenly. Drain and place in slow-cooking pot with remaining ingredients except cornstarch mixture and parsley. Cover and cook on low or high. Half-an-hour before serving, stir in the cornstarch mixture. Garnish with chopped parsley and serve with cooked noodles.

Low   8–10 hours
High   4–5 hours

Moussaka (Greece)

2 eggplants
⅓ cup oil
1 onion, chopped
1lb. ground chuck
salt and pepper
⅔ cup beef broth
3 tablespoons tomato paste
4 tomatoes, skinned
2 eggs
⅔ cup light cream
¼ cup grated Parmesan cheese

Slice the eggplants into ½-inch thick round slices. Fry lightly in the oil in a skillet. Drain on paper towels and arrange on the bottom of the slow-cooking pot. Fry the onion and beef until the beef is lightly browned. Drain excess fat and spread beef evenly over the eggplant. Season with salt and pepper. Mix broth and tomato paste and pour over the beef. Cover with a layer of sliced tomatoes. Beat the eggs, cream and cheese until well blended and pour evenly over the tomatoes. Cover and cook on low or high.

Low   4–6 hours
High   2–3 hours

ENTERTAINING

Entertaining is often curtailed because time is limited. With a little forward planning the slow-cooking pot can help you give a dinner party on any day of the week. At the end of this section there are two simple dinner party menus, using recipes in the book, plus a timetable to help you with the planning. The slow-cooking pot is left to cook the main dish, requiring little or no attention once it is switched on, leaving the hostess more time to lay the table and add the final touches to the other courses.

Parties always get off to a good start with a hot punch—Halloween punch (see page 116) has a delicious sting in its tail, so be sure to have extra supplies ready.

Use the slow-cooking pot as your buffet party center piece, filled with a hot dish such as a curry or perhaps a savory dip. Once cooked, the food can be kept hot on the low setting so that latecomers needn't be left out.

Cheese and wine parties are always popular, so why not treat your guests to a rich, creamy cheese fondue?

On a less sophisticated scale, the slow-cooking pot can be left to cook a simple supper dish to entertain your friends after the theater or simply to provide 'instant' hot soup when the baseball team is brought home after the match.

Opposite: Dinner menu 1 (page 118)

Halloween punch

A Halloween party would not be complete without a hot punch. Use the slow-cooking pot as the party center piece.

rind of 1 orange and 1 lemon
$\frac{1}{3}$ cup firmly packed brown sugar
2 teaspoons pumpkin pie spice
$7\frac{1}{2}$ cups red wine (claret, port)
$\frac{1}{2}$ cup brandy
2 small oranges, studded with whole cloves

Place all the ingredients in the slow-cooking pot. Cover and heat on high. Turn to low to keep hot.

High   1 hour

Spiced fruit punch

1 bottle (1 quart) port or sherry
$\frac{2}{3}$ cup orange juice
$\frac{2}{3}$ cup pineapple juice
3 tablespoons firmly packed brown sugar
rind and juice of 1 lemon
1 orange, sliced
4 canned pineapple slices, drained
2 teaspoons pumpkin pie spice

Place all the ingredients in the slow-cooking pot. Cover and heat on high, turn to low to keep hot.

High   1–2 hours

Curry dip

2 tablespoons lard or vegetable shortening
1 medium-sized onion, chopped
1 green pepper, seeded and chopped
1lb. ground chuck
2 tablespoons curry powder
1 tablespoon all-purpose flour
1 teaspoon chili powder
2 tablespoons tomato paste
1 apple, peeled, cored and chopped
$\frac{1}{4}$ cup raisins
1 tablespoon chutney
1 tablespoon lemon juice
salt and pepper
5 cups beef broth
fried onion rings and parsley to garnish

Heat the lard in a skillet and fry the onion and green pepper until they both begin to soften. Drain and place in the slow-cooking pot. Brown the beef in the skillet quickly. Drain excess fat, then stir in curry

powder, flour, chili and tomato paste. Stir well and add to the pot. Add remaining ingredients and stir well. Cover and cook on low or high. Adjust consistency if necessary with a little cornstarch mixed with water. Garnish with fried onion rings and a little parsley. Serve with crusty French bread or crackers.

Low   4–6 hours
High   2–3 hours

Cider cup

5 cups hard cider
$\frac{1}{3}$ cup firmly packed brown sugar
rind and juice of 1 lemon
few whole cloves
2 apples, cored and thickly sliced

Place the cider, sugar, lemon rind and juice in the slow-cooking pot. Press the cloves into the apple and float on top of the cider. Cover and heat on high, turn to low to keep hot.

High   1–2 hours

Seafood dip

2 cans ($10\frac{3}{4}$oz. each) condensed cream of shrimp soup
1 can (7oz.) tuna, drained and flaked
1 cup cooked, shelled and deveined shrimp
1 can (6oz.) chopped clams, drained
1 teaspoon chopped parsley
1 teaspoon Worcestershire sauce
salt and pepper

Empty soup into the slow-cooking pot and cook on high. Stir in the tuna, shrimp, clams, parsley and Worcestershire sauce, season to taste with salt and pepper. Cover and cook on high, turn to low to keep hot. Serve with slices of French bread, toast or plain crackers.

High   1 hour *plus* $\frac{1}{2}$ hour
Low   to keep warm

Tangy tomato juice

3lbs. tomatoes, washed
$\frac{1}{4}$ cup chopped onion
2 tablespoons lemon juice
4 tablespoons orange juice
$1\frac{1}{2}$ teaspoons sugar
1 teaspoon salt
finely grated rind of 1 orange
1 teaspoon Worcestershire sauce

few drops hot pepper sauce
chopped mint to garnish

Core and chop the tomatoes. Place tomatoes and onion in slow-cooking pot. Cover and cook on low. Press through a strainer. Return purée to slow-cooking pot and cook on high. Add lemon and orange juice, sugar, salt, orange rind, Worcestershire sauce and hot pepper sauce. Cook on high for a further 10 minutes. Chill before serving. Serve garnished with chopped mint.

Low 8–10 hours *then*
High 30 minutes
         plus 10 minutes

Fondue

1 clove garlic
3 cups ($\frac{3}{4}$lb.) grated Emmental cheese
3 cups ($\frac{3}{4}$lb.) grated Gruyère cheese
2 teaspoons all-purpose flour
2 cups dry white wine
1 teaspoon lemon juice
$\frac{1}{4}$ cup Kirsch (optional)
dash grated nutmeg
$\frac{1}{8}$ teaspoon black pepper
French bread cubes

Rub the inside of the slow-cooking pot with garlic. Mix the cheeses with the flour and place in the pot with the wine, lemon juice, Kirsch, nutmeg and black pepper. Cover and cook on low, stirring occasionally. (The fondue should be of a creamy consistency.) Keep hot and serve with cubes of French bread.

Low   3–4 hours

Dinner party menus

Menu 1

Pâté de foie de volaille

Rich beef casserole
Boiled or new potatoes
Broccoli
Baby carrots

Chocolate dessert

Day 1
Make pâté (see recipe page 49). Cool, cover with clean foil or wax paper and refrigerate in container.
Day 2
1 Make Chocolate dessert (see recipe page 97). Cool and refrigerate in container.

2 Grate a little plain chocolate for decoration, store in an air-tight container in the refrigerator.
3 Prepare all the ingredients for Rich beef casserole (see recipe page 55). Place in covered containers in the refrigerator.
4 Prepare accompanying vegetables.
Day 3
1 Begin cooking Rich beef casserole.
2 Prepare salad ingredients to garnish pâté, e.g. tomatoes, cucumber, lettuce. Store in covered containers in refrigerator.
3 Turn out pâté on to serving dish (dip container in hot water to help its release). Re-cover and refrigerate.
4 If serving red wine, allow to come to room temperature then open bottles 15 minutes before serving.
5 Thicken sauce of casserole. Keep hot on low setting.
6 Cook accompanying vegetables. Serve potatoes with a little butter and chopped parsley.
7 Turn out Chocolate dessert, decorate with whipped cream and grated chocolate. Chill again.
8 Garnish pâté. Make toast.

Menu 2

French onion soup

Pork tenderloin in sherry
Boiled rice
Zucchini
Broiled tomato halves

Crème caramel with cream

Day 1
Make the soup (see recipe page 13) but do not add the bread topping. Cool, cover and refrigerate.
Day 2
1 Make Crème caramel (see recipe page 92), cool and refrigerate in the cups.
2 Prepare all ingredients for Pork tenderloin in sherry (see recipe page 66). Place in covered containers in refrigerator.
3 Prepare zucchini and tomato halves. Store in airtight containers or plastic bags in the refrigerator.
4 Grate the cheese for soup topping.
Day 3
1 Begin cooking pork tenderloin.
2 Chill wine – white or rosé.
3 Turn out Crème caramel, allowing cups to drain over custards for several minutes to obtain all the caramel sauce.
4 Thicken the sauce in the slow-cooking pot. Keep hot on low setting.
5 Cook rice and vegetables.
6 Re-heat soup. Pour into a hot serving dish or tureen. Add rounds of French bread and cheese.
7 Garnish pork with cream and paprika.

WHAT ELSE?

Why not use the slow-cooking pot to warm rolls and Danish pastries, and make garlic bread. Heat rolls and pastries in the covered pot on high ½—1 hour. For garlic bread, crush a small clove of garlic and blend with ¼ cup butter. Slice a small French loaf and spread each slice with garlic butter. Put the slices together, wrap the loaf in foil. Heat on high ½—1 hour.

Frozen stews, casseroles or pies can be re-heated in their foil containers. They MUST have been thoroughly cooked and cooled quickly prior to freezing. Heat on low 4—8 hours or high 2—4 hours (with ⅔ cup water added to the pot), depending on weight and shape.

Slow-cooking jams

The low temperatures of the slow-cooking pot make it very suitable for softening fruit for jam making. The slowness of cooking combined with the small amount of liquid allows maximum extraction of the pectin while retaining the color and flavor of the fruit.

Apricots, gooseberries, black and red currants, cooking apples with blackberries or plums can all be used for the following recipe. Berries like raspberries and strawberries should have the liquid reduced by half.

2lbs. prepared fruit
$1\frac{1}{4}$ cups water
4 cups sugar

Put the prepared fruit and water in the slow-cooking pot. For pitted fruits like apricots and plums, cut in half, remove the pits and tie pits in a small piece of cheesecloth. Cook with the fruit and water, but remove before boiling with sugar. Cover and cook on low. Transfer the fruit and liquid to a large saucepan, add sugar and stir well over low heat until the sugar is thoroughly dissolved. Bring rapidly to a boil and boil until correct thickness is reached, about 5–15 minutes. Pour into sterilized jam jars, cover with melted paraffin and a lid.

Yield: About three $\frac{1}{2}$-pint jars
Low   8 hours or overnight

Slow-cooking Seville marmalade

2lbs. Seville oranges
2 lemons
5 cups boiling water
8 cups sugar

Cut the oranges and lemons in half; remove and reserve seeds from both. Slice the fruit thinly and place in the slow-cooking pot with $2\frac{1}{2}$ cups water. Cover and cook on low.

Simmer the seeds in remaining water for about 30 minutes. Strain the liquid from the seeds into a large saucepan. Add all the fruit and the liquid from the pot. Bring to a boil, add the sugar and stir over low heat until the sugar is completely dissolved. Boil rapidly until setting point is reached or until a small amount dropped onto a plate sets into a jelly. Test for a set after 15 minutes. Skim foam if necessary, allow to stand until a skin forms then pour into sterilized jelly jars, covering each one immediately with melted paraffin. Cover, label and store when cold in a cool, dry place.

Yield: Eight $\frac{1}{2}$-pint jars
Low   6–8 hours or overnight

Re-heating frozen cooked meals

Any dishes to be re-heated by this method must previously have been thoroughly cooked and then cooled and frozen as quickly as possible. Stews, casseroles, pies, etc. must be re-heated in their foil containers and have $\frac{2}{3}$ cup water poured around them. Heat on low or high, depending on the weight and shape of the food. A foil-wrapped parcel of a frozen vegetable, such as peas or beans, can be heated at the same time. Add a little salt and piece of butter to the vegetables.

Low   4–8 hours
High   2–4 hours

Chestnuts for Christmas

Pour boiling water over chestnuts, leave for 2 minutes, drain and remove skins. Place in the slow-cooking pot, cover with fresh water and cook on low. Chop or blend them for chestnut stuffing, or leave whole and mix with Brussels sprouts.

Low   3–4 hours

Corn and pepper relish

2 cans (11oz. each) kernel corn, drained
3 green peppers, seeded and chopped
1 onion, finely chopped
1 cucumber, chopped
2 tomatoes, chopped
$\frac{2}{3}$ cup cider vinegar
$\frac{3}{4}$ cup sugar
$\frac{1}{2}$ teaspoon salt
1 tablespoon celery salt
1 teaspoon mustard seed
1 teaspoon turmeric

Combine all the ingredients in the slow-cooking pot. Cover and cook on low or high. Remove cover, stir ingredients and continue cooking on high, *uncovered*. (This will thicken the relish.) Transfer hot relish to hot sterilized jars and seal immediately. Store in refrigerator; use within 2–3 weeks. Makes an ideal accompaniment to cold meats, with salad, or as a barbecue side dish.

Yield: Three ½-pints
Low   6 hours
High   3 hours *plus*
High   1 hour

Oatmeal

oil or butter for greasing
1 cup Scotch coarse oatmeal
3¾ cups cold water
¼ teaspoon salt
milk or cream
sugar to taste

Lightly grease the slow-cooking pot. Mix together the oatmeal, water and salt in the pot. Cover and cook on low. Stir thoroughly before serving, add cream and sugar to taste.

Low   6–8 hours or overnight

Banana chutney

½lb. onions, chopped
1½ cups chopped, pitted dates
6 bananas, mashed
1¼ cups vinegar
½ cup chopped crystallized ginger
salt
1½ cups raisins
½ cup firmly packed brown sugar

Place all the ingredients in the slow-cooking pot and stir well. Cover and cook on high until all ingredients are cooked. Stir well and continue cooking *uncovered* on high to allow chutney to thicken.

Yield: Three ½-pint jars
High   3 hours *plus* 1 hour

Green tomato chutney

When you have an abundance of green tomatoes in the garden and you cannot eat them quickly enough, make this tangy chutney for your shelves.

3lbs. green tomatoes, chopped

2 small cooking apples, peeled, cored and chopped
2 medium-sized onions
¼ cup whole pickling spice (tied in a piece of cheesecloth)
½ cup firmly packed brown sugar
2 cups malt vinegar
2 teaspoons salt

Place tomatoes, apples and onions in the slow-cooking pot with remaining ingredients and stir well. Cover and cook on low until all ingredients are tender and chutney is thick. Remove the spice, pour the chutney into sterilized jars and cover at once.

Yield: 3 pints
Low   8–10 hours or overnight

Below: Yogurt

Yogurt

This can only be made in a stoneware pot that can be removed from base.

1 quart homogenized milk
4 teaspoons plain yogurt
4 teaspoons sugar (optional)

Heat the milk in a saucepan until just warm; if the milk is too hot at this point it will destroy the yogurt culture and the mix will not set. Put the yogurt in the slow-cooking pot and stir in the sugar and milk thoroughly. Cover with a clean dish towel (do *not* add the pot cover). Heat on low then turn off the pot and leave undisturbed for 2 hours. The yogurt should now be just set. Lift the pot from base, cool then refrigerate.

Low   1 hour

Flavorings
Chopped fruit or nuts should be added after the yogurt has set.
    Powdered milk drink flavorings are ideal to

use: allow about 2—3 teaspoons to flavor the basic recipe.

Powdered coffee or cocoa may be used: allow 2—3 teaspoons to flavor the basic recipe.

Omit the sugar given in the basic recipe and stir in honey or brown sugar to taste after the yogurt has set.

Spiced fruit loaf

2 cups self-rising flour
pinch of salt
6 tablespoons butter or margarine

¾ cup chopped mixed candied fruit
¼ cup firmly packed brown sugar
½ teaspoon pumpkin pie spice
½ cup chopped walnuts
1 large egg, beaten
milk
light brown sugar

Pre-heat slow-cooking pot on high for 15 minutes. Sift flour and salt, cut in butter until mixture resembles fine breadcrumbs. Add the fruit, sugar, spice and nuts. Mix with the egg and enough milk until the consistency of muffin batter. Transfer mixture to a greased 2-cup loaf pan. Cover with a double thickness of greased wax paper or aluminum

foil. Stand the container in the slow-cooking pot and pour 2½ cups boiling water around it. Cover and cook on high. When cooked, remove paper cover from pan, sprinkle the top liberally with brown sugar and broil until lightly browned. Unmold carefully when cool.

High   2½–3½ hours

Bran teabread

1 cup All-Bran
½ cup firmly packed brown sugar
1 cup mixed dried fruit

1¼ cups milk
1 cup self-rising flour

Mix together the All-Bran, sugar and dried fruit in a bowl. Stir in the milk and stand for 1 hour. Add the sifted flour and place the mixture in greased 2-cup loaf pan. Cover with greased aluminum foil or wax paper. Pre-heat slow-cooking pot on high for 15 minutes. Stand the pan in the pot and pour 2½ cups boiling water around it. Cover and cook on high. When cooked, remove paper immediately. Allow to cool before unmolding. When cold, slice and serve spread with butter.

High   2–3 hours

Index

Apple:
  Apple brown betty 98
  Apple and chocolate pudding 95
  Apple snowballs 94
  Baked apples 92
Apricot:
  Curried pork with apricots 68
Artichokes française 34
Asparagus oeufs en cocotte 108
Avocado, baked, with crab 23

Bacon:
  Leek and bacon pudding 36
  Liver and bacon 74
  Liver and bacon risotto 78
  West Country ham hocks 80
Banana:
  Banana chutney 123
  Caribbean bananas 106
Barbecued pork 68
Barbecued spareribs 106
Bean:
  Bean hotpot 84
  Beef 'n' bean casserole 56
  Boston baked beans 36
  Cassoulet 112
  Navy or pea beans with cheese 88
  Red bean braise 61
  Savory roast 84
  South Texas bean casserole 72
Beef:
  To roast beef 56
  Beef casserole 54
  Beef 'n' bean casserole 56
  Beef risotto 56
  Beef roulades 58
  Beef stroganoff 106
  Boeuf Catalan 104
  Boeuf flamande 105
  Boiled beef and dumplings 54
  Carbonnade of beef 58
  Chili-con-carne 106
  Cholent 62
  Chuck roast with vegetables 62
  Continental meat loaf 60
  Family shepherd's pie 56
  Farmer's beef stew with herby
    dumplings 58
  Fruit and vegetable curry 85
  Hungarian goulasch 104
  Lasagne 61
  Malayan beef and shrimp soup 104
  Meatballs in tomato sauce 58
  Moussaka 113
  Pot roast of beef 55
  Red bean braise 61
  Rich beef casserole 55
  Savory ground beef cobbler 55
  South Texas bean casserole 72
  Steak and kidney pie 54
  Stiffado 105
  Top round braise 61

Beef stroganoff 106
Beets:
  Borscht 16
Blueberry streusel cake 96
Boeuf Catalan 104
Boeuf flamande 105
Bolognese sauce 17
Borscht 16
Boston baked beans 36
Bouillabaisse 26; vegetarian 86
Bran teabread 125
Bread and butter pudding, orange 93
Bread pudding, old-fashioned 93
Broths 12
Butter baked whiting 20

Cabbage:
  Cabbage rolls 32
  Rice roulades 86
  Sweet and sour red cabbage 32
Cake:
  Blueberry streusel cake 96
  Chocolate pear upside-down cake 99
Canneloni, vegetable 88
Cantonese dinner 110
Carbonnade of beef 58
Casseroles. See also Stews
  Beef casserole 54
  Beef 'n' bean casserole 56
  Cheese and potato casserole 84
  Chicken casserole 44
  Coeur en casserole 77
  Continental fish casserole 20
  Cowboy casserole 60
  Mock-lobster casserole 24
  Pork casserole 70
  Rabbit casserole 46
  Rabbit and partridge casserole 48
  Rich beef casserole 55
  Sausage and vegetable casserole 61
  South Texas bean casserole 72
  Summer lamb casserole 64
  Vegetable casserole 32
  Welsh lamb casserole 66
  Woodman's casserole 49
Cassoulet 112
Castle puddings 92
Celeriac, sweet and sour 32
Celery:
  Braised celery 38
  Celery and cheese soufflé 38
  Celery and ham roulades 32
  Cream of celery soup 15
Cheese:
  Celery and cheese soufflé 38
  Cheese and potato casserole 84
  Cheese pudding 88
  Cheesy baked onions 88
  Cheesy fish bake 24
  Fondue 118
  Macaroni and cheese 85
  Navy or pea beans with cheese 88
  Savory roast 84
  Types to use in a slow cooking pot 8
Cherry:
  Duckling with cherries 47

Chestnuts, to cook 122
Chicken:
  Braised cider chicken 51
  Chicken broth 12
  Chicken cacciatore 42
  Chicken casserole 44
  Chicken curry 42
  Chicken noodle soup 16
  Chicken in a pot 42
  Chicken and vegetable pie 44
  Chicken vindaloo 109
  Coq au vin 112
  Country chicken 44
  Fricassée fowl 42
  Lemon baked chicken 44
  Mexican chicken 105
  Oriental chicken 51
  Poussin Véronique 45
  Roast chicken 42
  Sesame chicken 112
  Winter chicken with dumplings 51
Chili-con-carne 106
Chocolate:
  Apple and chocolate pudding 95
  Chocolate dessert 97
  Chocolate pear upside-down cake 99
  Spiced chocolate chip puddings 98
Cholent 62
Chuck roast with vegetables 62
Christmas pudding, English 100
Chutney:
  Banana chutney 123
  Green tomato chutney 122
Cider cup 118
Cock-a-leekie 16
Cod:
  Mock-lobster casserole 24
  Rice stuffed cod 20
Coq au vin 112
Corn:
  Corn-on-the-cob 36
  Corn and pepper relish 122
  Tuna and corn savory 20
  Country vegetable soup 12
Crab:
  Baked avocado with crab 24
Crème brûlée 98
Crème caramel 92
Cucumber soup, iced 14
Cup custards 92
Curried dishes:
  Chicken curry 42
  Chicken vindaloo 109
  Curried lamb 65
  Curried pork with apricots 68
  Curried shrimp 20
  Curry dip 116
  Curry sauce 16
  Fruit and vegetable curry 85

Date pudding 99
Desserts. See also Puddings
  Apple brown betty 98
  Apple and chocolate pudding 95
  Apple snowballs 94
  Baked apples 92

Caribbean bananas 106
Castle puddings 92
Chinese pears 105
Chocolate dessert 97
Crème brûlée 98
Crème caramel 92
Cup custards 92
Date pudding 99
English Christmas pudding 100
Figs with wine and honey 106
Fruit compote 96
Lemon pudding 98
Old-fashioned bread pudding 93
Orange bread and butter pudding 93
Peach flambé 98
Pears in red wine 95
Pineapple upside-down cake 94
Raisin pudding 92
Rhubarb 94
Rice pudding 92
Spiced chocolate chip puddings 98
Stewed fruit 94
Summer pudding 96
Deviled herrings 22
Dinner menus 118
Dips:
    Curry dip 116
    Seafood dip 116
Drinks:
    Cider cup 118
    Halloween punch 116
    Spiced fruit punch 116
Duck à l'orange 48
Duckling with cherries 47
Dumplings, 51, 54; herby 58

Eggplant:
    Eggplant florentine 37
    Stuffed eggplants 86
Egg:
    Eggs florentine 84
    Oeufs en cocotte 108
Endive, braised 34
Espagnole sauce 17

Fennel and potato 36
Figs with wine and honey 106
Fish. See also Cod, Haddock etc.
    Bouillabaisse 26
    Cheesy fish bake 24
    Continental fish casserole 20
    Fish pie 23
    Fish broth 12
    Seafood chowder 14
Flounder bonne femme 23
Flounder parcels 21
Fondue 118
Fricassée of rabbit 46
Fruit. See also Apple, Apricot, etc.
    Family fruit pie 100
    Fruit compote 96
    Fruit and vegetable curry 85
    Spiced fruit loaf 124
    Stewed fruit 94

Game. See Hare, Partridge, etc.

Game hens with grapes 49
Gravy, to thicken 8

Haddock:
    Fish oeuf en cocotte 108
    Kedgeree 26
Halloween punch 116
Ham:
    Boiled ham to serve cold 74
    Celery and ham roulades 32
    Split pea and ham soup 12
    West Country ham hocks 80
    William's ham 78
Hare, braised 45
Heart:
    Coeur en casserole 77
    Stuffed lambs' hearts 64
Heat settings 7
Herbs and spices 8
Herring:
    Deviled herrings 22
    Somerset herrings 26
    Soused herrings 20
Hungarian goulasch 104

Irish stew 64
Italian stuffed tomatoes 36
Italian vegetable soup 14

Jam 122

Kedgeree 26
Kidney:
    Kidney stew 80
    Kidneys turbigo 81
    Steak and kidney pie 54

Lamb and mutton:
    To roast lamb 56
    Braised orange lamb 65
    Curried lamb 65
    Farmhouse lamb 63
    Irish stew 64
    Lamb chops with mustard and
      horseradish 66
    Lamb provençale 64
    Lamb and zucchini roll 65
    Mutton stew 64
    Navarin of lamb 62
    Red-cooked lamb 108
    Scotch broth 15
    Summer lamb casserole 64
    Tomato brady 63
    Welsh lamb casserole 66
Lambs' hearts, stuffed 64
Lambs' tongues in piquant sauce 66
Lasagne 61
Leek and bacon pudding 36
Leek and potato soup 12
Lemon:
    Lemon baked chicken 44
    Lemon mackerel 21
    Lemon pudding 98
Lentil soup 16; stew 88
Liquids for cooking 8
Liver:

Country-style pâté 75
Liver and bacon 74
Liver and bacon risotto 78
Liver and tomato pâté 49
Liver with sage sauce 75
Roman liver 77
Topped liver 78

Macaroni and cheese 85
Mackerel:
    Lemon mackerel 21
    Mackerel loaf 22
    Tomato and mackerel bake 24
Marmalade 122
Meat. See also Beef etc.
    To prepare meat 8
    To roast joints of meat 56
    Continental meat loaf 60
    Meat broth 12
    Meatballs in tomato sauce 58
Minestrone 14
Mock-lobster casserole 24
Moussaka 113
Mullet:
    Mediterranean mullet 24
Mulligatawny 15
Mushroom:
    Veal with mushrooms 72
Mutton. See Lamb and mutton

Navarin of lamb 62
Navy or pea beans with cheese 88
Nut rice 86

Oatmeal 123
Oeufs en cocotte 108
Onion:
    Cheesy baked onions 88
    French onion soup 13
Orange:
    Braised orange lamb 65
    Duck à l'orange 48
    Orange bread and butter pudding 93
    Pork chops with orange 69
    Red snapper with orange 21
Osso bucco 108
Ox tongue 78
Oxtail:
    Braised oxtail 54
    Oxtail ragoût 78

Paella 110
Parsley sauce 80
Partridge in red wine 50
Pasta, to use in slow-cooking pot 8
Pâté:
    Country-style pâté 75
    Liver and tomato pâté 49
    Pâté de foie de volaille 49
Peach flambé 98
Pear:
    Chinese pears 105
    Chocolate pear upside-down cake 99
    Pears in red wine 95
Pepper:
    Stuffed green peppers 34

Pheasant, braised 50
Pies:
    Chicken and vegetable pie 44
    Family fruit pie 100
    Family shepherd's pie 56
    Fish pie 23
    Rabbit pie 45
    Steak and kidney pie 54
Pigeon:
    Woodman's casserole 49
Pineapple glazed ribs 70
Pineapple upside-down cake 94
Pork:
    To roast pork 56
    Barbecued pork 68
    Barbecued spareribs 106
    Braised pork chops 68
    Cantonese dinner 110
    Curried pork with apricots 68
    Hungarian pork 69
    Old-fashioned smoked pork
    dinner 74
    Pineapple glazed ribs 70
    Pork birds 72
    Pork casserole 70
    Pork chops in cider 69
    Pork chops with orange 69
    Pork chops with rice 70
    Pork tenderloin in sherry 66
    Sweet and sour pork 109
Potato:
    Cheese and potato casserole 84
    Fennel and potato 36
    Leek and potato soup 12
Poultry. See Chicken etc.
Poussin Véronique 45
Puddings, savory:
    Cheese pudding 88
    Leek and bacon pudding 36
Punch 116

Rabbit:
    Rabbit casserole 46
    Rabbit fricassée 46
    Rabbit with mustard 46
    Rabbit and partridge casserole 48
    Rabbit pie 45
Raisin pudding 92
Ratatouille 34
Red cabbage, sweet and sour 32
Red-cooked lamb 108
Red snapper with orange 21
Re-heating 122
Rhubarb 94
Rice:
    Beef risotto 56
    Fried rice 51
    Liver and bacon risotto 78
    Nut rice 86
    Paella 110
    Pork chops with rice 70
    Rice pudding 92
    Rice roulades 86
    Rice stuffed cod 20
    Savory rice 84
    Tuna pilaf 26

Types to use 8
Rich beef casserole 55

Sauces:
    To thicken sauces 8
    Bolognese sauce 17
    Curry sauce 16
    Espagnole sauce 17
    Parsley sauce 80
    Tomato sauce 17
Sausage:
    Cowboy casserole 60
    Sausage and vegetable casserole 61
Seafood dip 116
Sesame chicken 112
Shepherd's pie 56
Shrimp:
    Curried shrimp 20
    Malayan beef and shrimp soup 104
Soufflé:
    Celery and cheese soufflé 38
Soups:
    To use as cooking liquid 8
    Borscht 16
    Bouillabaisse 26; vegetarian 86
    Chicken noodle soup 16
    Cock-a-leekie 16
    Country vegetable soup 12
    Cream of celery soup 15
    Cream of tomato soup 13
    French onion soup 13
    Iced cucumber soup 14
    Italian vegetable soup 14
    Leek and potato soup 12
    Lentil soup 16
    Malayan beef and shrimp soup 104
    Minestrone 14
    Mulligatawny 15
    Scotch broth 15
    Seafood chowder 14
    Split pea and ham soup 12
Soused herrings 20
South Texas bean casserole 72
Spiced fruit loaf 124
Spiced fruit punch 116
Spinach:
    Eggs florentine 84
    Spinach castles 85
Squash:
    Stuffed acorn squash 37
    Stuffed summer squash 34
Steak and kidney pie 54
Stews: See also Casseroles
    Farmer's beef stew with herby
    dumplings 58
    Irish stew 64
    Kidney stew 80
    Lentil stew 88
    Mutton stew 64
Stiffado 105
Stuffed acorn squash 37
Stuffed eggplants 86
Stuffed green peppers 34
Stuffed lambs' hearts 64
Stuffed summer squash 34
Stuffed veal 72

Stuffed veal shoulder 70
Stuffed zucchini 38
Summer pudding 96
Sweet and sour celeriac 32
Sweet and sour pork 109
Sweet and sour red cabbage 32

Tangy tomato juice 116
Teabread:
    Bran teabread 125
    Spiced fruit loaf 124
Thickening 8
Timing 7
Tomato:
    Cream of tomato soup 13
    Green tomato chutney 123
    Italian stuffed tomatoes 36
    Meatballs in tomato sauce 58
    Tangy tomato juice 116
    Tomato brady 63
    Tomato and mackerel bake 24
    Tomato oeufs en cocotte 108
    Tomato sauce 17
Tongue:
    Cold tongue 80
    Lambs' tongues in piquant sauce 66
Tripe with parsley sauce 80
Trout, baked, with almonds 24
Tuna:
    Tuna and corn savory 20
    Tuna loaf 22
    Tuna pilaf 26
Turkey in Madeira 47
Turkey roll 46

Using a slow-cooking pot 7

Varieties of slow-cooking pots 9
Veal:
    Osso bucco 108
    Stuffed veal 72
    Stuffed veal shoulder 70
    Veal chops Magyar 70
    Veal in Marsala 112
    Veal or pork birds 72
    Veal suprême 74
    Veal with mushrooms 72
Vegetables. See also Artichoke etc.
    To choose and prepare vegetables 8
    Chicken and vegetable pie 44
    Country vegetable soup 12
    Fruit and vegetable curry 85
    Italian vegetable soup 14
    Ratatouille 34
    Sausage and vegetable casserole 61
    Vegetable canneloni 88
    Vegetable casserole 32

Whiting, butter baked 20

Yogurt 123

Zucchini:
    Lamb and zucchini roll 65
    Stuffed zucchini 38
    Zucchini provençale 38